Trammels, Trenchers, and Tartlets

Trammels, Trenchers, and Tartlets

Joyce W. Carlo

PEREGRINE PRESS, Publishers
Old Saybrook, Connecticut

Cover design by Frank Westerberg

Book design by Hildebrandt Associates

Manufactured in the United States of America

First Printing

ISBN 0-933614-13-6

Table of Contents

Acknowledgements

It is a very real pleasure for me to acknowledge the help and cooperation I have received from others during the writing of this book. I am grateful to those who opened the doors to their historic houses and their collections, as well as the doors to their minds. It has been a stimulating and a humbling experience to meet and talk with these people, to whom I say a most sincere thank you.

Ruth Briggs, late Curator-Emeritus of the Plymouth Antiquarian Society

Carla Crowley, former Curator, Plymouth Antiquarian Society

James Baker, Research Librarian, Plimoth Plantation

David Dangremond, Director, Webb-Deane-Stevens Museum, Wethersfield, Connecticut.

Mrs. James Newton, Curator, Whipple House, Ipswich, Massachusetts.

Charles Miller, Chairman, Wells-Shipman-Ward House, South Glastonbury, Connecticut.

Janice Riemer, former Director, The Farmington Museum/ Stanley-Whitman House, Farmington, Connecticut.

I have used materials at the Henry N. Flynt Library, Historic Deerfield, Massachusetts; The American Antiquarian Society, Worcester, Massachusetts; the Connecticut Historical Society and the State Library, Hartford, Connecticut; and the Litchfield Historical Society, Litchfield, Connecticut. For this privilege I am grateful.

Thanks also to my friends at home:
June Giannaccio for the art work,
Jane Lewis for testing the recipes,
Alice Terrill for her notes and recipes,
Michael Colligan, Chairman of the History Department,
    St. Margaret's-McTernan School, Waterbury, for reading
    the manuscript with the historian's eye,
Robert Gallucci for a million library services.
And to Andy and Elizabeth, thanks for enduring Mom's project.

J.W.C.
Watertown, Connecticut

A Note on Terms

The room we designate a kitchen has been called a variety of names. Rhode Island houses of the seventeenth century have what is called the *fire room*, the room with the cooking fireplace. In the central-chimney houses of Connecticut and Massachusetts the word *hall* refers to the cooking-dining-everything room (while the entry, which we would call the *front hall*, is the *porch*). *Keeping-room* applies more to the kitchen in the lean-to, but is frequently used also for what we have just said was the hall. When ells were added, the names *Great Kitchen*, *Little Kitchen*, and *Summer Kitchen* came into use. I have chosen to call the room where the cooking fireplace was located the *kitchen*.

Plimoth refers to the reconstructed Pilgrim Village incorporated as Plimoth Plantation. I use *Plymouth* for the original settlement and the modern town.

As for the term *housewife*, it refers to a noble occupation and I use it with respect.

Preface

If it is true that in the heart-of-hearts of every American, his roots are in New England, then it follows that "home" is best symbolized by a weathered salt-box house in a quiet village setting or by an ocean-side shingled cottage behind its hollyhocks. Americans long for the sight of these houses and make pilgrimages to them as if they were shrines to home. The imagined aroma of baked beans, brown bread, and pumpkin pie is like incense, and we picture some sort of Eden-before-the-Fall life in this pre-Revolutionary New England.

Looking at the serene survivals of colonial days, it is hard to imagine life in them as anything but content. We sense there was no frantic rush urging colonial housewives on to one activity after another. They seem to have had time to really enjoy their homes and families, to wander over fields picking berries, to embroider their samplers and crewel bedspreads, to take homemade breads from oven to table. And though we have heard about privation, cold, disease and early death, we cannot comprehend them. They are not part of the cherished picture. How can we look across a meadow bursting with the bloom of purple loosestrife to Rebecca Nurse's red house resting in its dooryard herb garden and conceive of the life there for that woman grown old in housewifery suddenly accused of witchcraft? We cannot.

If there is any way toward a vicarious experience of our colonial sister's life, it has to be by way of the hearth, for here was the heart of her home, and the center of her earthly life.

Like looking long at a picture of a far-away relative or dear friend in hopes of springing her back to life, we can look long at the old fireplaces of New England and make life around them become real. Maybe by looking hard enough at the heart of their homes, we can share with some sense of reality the experiences of the women who lived in them, those housewives whose courage and stamina we can never match, whose toil at the open hearth in frontier settlements we can admire, but never duplicate.

THE HOUSE

The earliest English shelters clinging desperately to the Massachusetts coast were not at all the picturesque saltbox houses that we see nestled so cozily into the New England landscape today. The saltbox was, in house generations, two removed from what one uprooted Englishman, Edward Johnson, called "wigwams, huts, and hovels that the English dwelt in at their first coming."[1]

Those colonizing Englishmen, most of them cultivated and educated, all of them ambitious, would not long be content with such housing. As soon as possible they replaced the first shelters with something resembling home. It took only a season in Rhode Island, where "as winter came on the new Plantation of Providence began to have more substantial dwellings, akin to . . . an 'English house.'"[2] By 1642, Johnson could proudly and gratefully report that "The Lord hath been pleased to turn [those early hovels] . . . into orderly, fair and well-built houses, well furnished many of them."[3]

The first homes erected were simple, frequently one room with loft. None of these remain except where incorporated into a much enlarged house that grew from additions to the first. There are, however, reconstructions of the originals at Salem's Pioneer Village and at Plimoth Plantation.

6

At Plimoth much fastidious research has led to the recreation of a life syle we find hard to fit into our idealized view of Pilgrims and First Thanksgiving. The Billington house there is the most nearly authentic to the first year according to latest research.

It has a dirt floor, a chimney made of logs covered with clay, and a jambless fireplace with a shield, or curtain of linen sailcloth, to encourage the smoke up the chimney instead of into the room. This room is not quaint; it is realistic. It is a hovel, as Johnson said. A recent tourist poked her head in and surmised, in the absence of a guide, "This must have been where they kept the animals."

The houses at Plimoth do look crude, but with a meal cooking over the fire and an enthusiastic modern Pilgrim lending life to the setting by telling us in her learned dialect why she left England for the New World, we begin to see the Pilgrim home of the first decade. Essentially it is a room enclosing a fireplace, and that fireplace is a family gathering place providing warmth, light and meals for the household.

In Rhode Island early houses were "stone-ended," one-room-plus-loft structures with a fireplace whose great stone chimney formed one whole wall. North of Boston the style was called a "one-room, two-story cottage," again with the fireplace focus of the whole. In all cases the fireplace is the essential, the starting point, and the house seems to exist only as an enclosure for this sanctum.

But that enclosure was home to these pioneers who "knew they were pilgrims"[4] on a holy trip into a strange land. In England, home had been not a wigwam, but a rural cottage or house usually medieval in structure and feeling. Even the adventurers among them (those who crossed the ocean for other than religious reasons and held no quarrel with the Anglican Church) shared a common view of "home" —of thatched roofs, of stout timbers, of leaded casement windows, of upper stories that projected over the first. Put these people down in a "howling wilderness" with no one to help them but each other, and is it any wonder that the homes built in the New World should bear a strong family resemblance to homes of Old England? They did not try to innovate but to re-create the loved and the familiar. They reconstructed medieval England in New England.

The Stanley-Whitman House, 1660.

The Pilgrims at Plimoth and the first Puritans at the Bay Colony put thatched roofs on their one-room homes. It took but a short time for them to realize that New England's summers are hotter and dryer than Old England's and can create a great fire hazard for dried thatch. In winter the New England nor'easters buried it with more snow than it could support. Fortunately, wood was plentiful here and all it took to produce a shingled roof was a man's labor so that within seven years of settlement, the Plymouth Court outlawed the use of thatch. In the Bay Colony gables were favored on larger frame houses, giving more interior space on the second floor and more light from their windows. We see them on the famous House of the Seven Gables, which started as a house of three gables. But gables, too, were eventually abandoned as impractical in New England's bitter winters.

Many early houses were built with a second story overhang, which some authorities believe was contrived for gaining more second floor living space in old England's crowded town houses. Others call it an aid in fighting Indians, but since the style originated in England, where there was no threat from Indians, it is hard to accept this explanation. Actually the overhang would afford an Indian a point of immunity and safety from which to wreak his havoc. These over-hangs, with their decorative pendants and brackets, were also abandoned as people ceased copying old home models and adopted new. The overhang style can be seen at the Parson Capen House (1683) in Topsfield and the Ironmaster's House (1650) in Saugus, both in Massachusetts, and at the Stanley-Whitman House (1660) in Farmington and the Buttolph-Williams (1692) in Wethersfield, Connecticut.

The Henry Whitfield House (1639) in Guilford, Connecticut, is considered the oldest stone house in New England, and it fits none of these descriptions. Although the party led by the Rev. Mr. Whitfield to the New World came mostly from Surrey, where half-timbered houses were the style, here was built a completely different kind of structure. William Leete of Cambridge, later to become leader of New Haven Colony, may have imposed his home architecture on the group, for the house resembles the Cotswold cottages west of London, where one can find stonework and chimneys almost identical to the Whitfield House. This house was a garrison and meeting house for 25 families as well as home for the Whitfields and their nine children and several servants. Its stone walls are two feet thick and, in the

Decorative pendant, Stanley-Whitman House.

medieval tradition, it has a great hall 30′ by 15′ with a fireplace on the outer walls at each end.[5]

When it came time to enlarge, the one-room plan could be duplicated easily on the other side of the chimney, thereby doubling the size of the house and putting the source of heat in its center. In the Massachusetts Bay this seems to have been a common practice. The John Balch House (1636) in Beverly was a one-over-one-room house until 1650, when John's son Benjamin enlarged it to a central-chimney, two-over-two-rooms house, possibly (or probably) because Mrs. Balch had borne him 13 children. In Newbury, the large, rambling Tristram Coffin House began life about 1653 as a one-room-plus-loft. When son Nathaniel brought his bride home in 1693, it received its first addition toward the east, and in the next generation Joseph and his bride built toward the northeast. Fourth generation Joshua also had to build "considering my family increases so fast."[6] Up in Newbury, Stephen Swett lived in a hogan on the banks of the Parker River for 20 years before receiving a grant of land where he finally built his two-story, one-room cottage, completed in 1670, and doubled in size in 1720.

Often the central-chimney house was built initially as a complete unit and, indeed, the builders of the half-houses may have known exactly what they were aiming for in their initial, partial building. The Buttolph-Williams House (1692), is the classic central-chimney, two-over-two rooms house. It stands weathered and unadorned, speaking to us of the beauty to be found in simplicity. The origin of this style was East Anglia, that seedbed of English Puritanism, but it was in New England that the style flourished and developed for over a hundred years before being replaced by one reflecting the greater ease and wealth of the late eighteenth century.

When the family needed to enlarge a four-room, central-chimney house, a lean-to could be built across the back and still that central chimney would be central and its hugeness would accommodate one more fireplace. This is the classic saltbox house seen so much in all New England, especially in Massachusetts and Connecticut, chaste and sturdy, almost a symbol for the New England home. Its long sweep of roof gives protection from the north wind and its windows on the south catch every possible warming ray of the low-hanging winter sun.

This is the style of the Hyland House (1660 and 1720) in Guilford, Connecticut, where upstairs in the little room under the lean-to roof we can see the original clapboards and leaded window in what had been the outside wall of the 1660 house. The Jefferd's Tavern (1750) now in York, Maine, also received a lean-to addition, though its roof does not follow cleanly the slope of the main roof, and the Jackson House (1664) in Portsmouth, New Hampshire, has a lean-to built onto the narrow end of the house rather than across the rear. The Rebecca Nurse House in Danvers, Massachusetts, is another seventeenth century dwelling with a rear lean-to, but this one extends even beyond the house, resulting in an ell called the Beverly Jog. So it went, with house builders always adapting to new needs and tastes, but never straying far from familiar, traditional forms.

In the next development the plan of the first floor saltbox was duplicated on the second, thus eliminating the long sloping roof of the lean-to and providing two or three additional rooms upstairs. This is the style of the Governor Jonathan Trumbull Home (1740) in Lebanon and of the Wells-Shipman-Ward House (1755) in South Glastonbury, both Connecticut.

When growing fortunes demanded more luxury in a home, a builder could take the plan of that central-chimney, two-over-two house and build two of them facing each other with a spacious hall between, producing the more elegant home of the later eighteenth century. Among such central-hall homes in Connecticut are the Justice Oliver Ellsworth House (1740) in Windsor, the Webb House (1752) in Wethersfield (where Washington and Rochambeau planned the strategy that eventually ended the Revolution) and the Hale Homestead (1776) in Coventry.

Colonel Leffingwell of Norwich, Connecticut, did this one better. He put two saltboxes together at right angles to each other. The result is a bit confusing to the occasional visitor, but in its day it provided a commodious home and tavern for the wayfarer.

There were other individualistic variations in house style. The story-and-a-half cottage with its central chimney is found throughout New England, the modest home of a modest farmer or fisherman. The Jonathan Dickerman House (c. 1770) in Hamden, Connecticut, is such a house. This style finds its most beautiful expression on Cape Cod and the Islands of Nantucket and Martha's Vineyard. The Cape

Cod cottage has a central chimney and a room to right and left of the narrow front entry with its staircase, just as in the typical central-chimney house. Upstairs however, the rooms are directly under the roof and thus have sloping ceilings. The rear room downstairs is like the rear room in the typical lean-to house, but this house has no lean-to. The Cape Cod cottage was also built as a half-house or three-quarter-house. In the former, the entry hall and a room to only one side, with the rear room, constituted the main floor plan. In the three-quarter, one of the front rooms was only half the width of the other. The proportions of the Cape Cod cottage are so perfect that half, three-quarter, or full cottages are all equally pleasing to behold.

An early eighteenth century house that is a little out-of-the-ordinary is the Mission House in Stockbridge, Massachusetts. Although it fits none of these descriptions, it nevertheless appears from the outside to be another frame, central-hall house, for it has two chimneys and a front hall, which surprisingly does not lead through to the back. The stairs and the hall are wide, unlike most houses of its date. There is a room to both right and left of the hall, and each has a fireplace in its rear wall. What makes the difference is the long, rather narrow room that extends across the back, not under a lean-to but as part of the main house. Upstairs there are two front chambers each with a fireplace as in the rooms below, and to their rear are two small rooms and a passageway behind the chimneys.

The house was built in 1739 by John Sargeant, Yale graduate and tutor to the Stockbridge Indians. Mr. Sargeant wooed and won Abigail Williams, a lass who had grown up in Boston. Tradition says that she consented to marry Mr. Sargeant only if he provided as good a house as she was used to, and she would tolerate no Indians in her living quarters.

Whether or not this was the situation, she could have had no complaints about the house Mr. Sargeant provided for her. It was the first frame house erected in Stockbridge and not only was its floor plan unique but its panelling was elegant. In the parlor, the door with its rounded top matched exactly the door to the china cupboard, balancing perfectly the entire wall. Also, the bake oven and its ash receptacle below could be closed off when not in use by means of a door that matched the panelling. She had a fine fireplace for cooking, smaller than eastern Massachusetts fireplaces but equipped with a crane and a granite hearth, and the bake oven had its own separate flue. The room across the rear of the house was for the Reverend Mr. Sargeant to consult with Indians who called at the home but did not enter Mistress Sargeant's rooms.

In New London, Connecticut, some new architectural details were introduced by the exiled Acadians from Nova Scotia, thirty-five of whom were granted asylum there by Connecticut's governor, and employment by Captain Nathaniel Shaw. Captain Shaw had a frame house built on a granite ledge at water's edge. He had found good fortune in shipping, and a new house seemed in order. The Acadians built him a "mansion house" (1756) of stone quarried from his ledge. The style is central-hall but with outside-wall fireplaces, and instead of wood panelling his walls were made of mortar, shaped and stained to pass for beautiful panelling.

Trade and shipping made many eighteenth century New Englanders prosperous, and the contact these people had with other colonies and other countries gave them a cosmopolitan taste for style. In seacoast and river towns new homes reflected this prosperity and attitude. In turn, country squires who were wealthy enough copied the styles they saw on their infrequent trips to town or their annual terms in the colonial assemblies. The eighteenth century mansions of Salem and Portsmouth, Boston and Newport were trimmed down perhaps and sometimes poorly imitated, but nevertheless their Samuel McIntyre or Charles Bulfinch grace in style was brought to the interior.

On the other hand, we may find a house built brand new in 1800 in the old central-chimney style. Then we may suspect we are dealing with a reactionary Yankee, more in the minority but more celebrated in yarns than the true Yankee who imitated change in everything from mousetraps and clocks to systems of government.

Whatever the changes in the architecture of the house, in all of the houses, even that of the second president of the United States, there were few differences and few changes in the cooking fireplace. There were refinements in the placement of the bake oven and in the pole or crane from which the pots hung, but that was about all.

Mrs. John Adams and her maid prepared the family meals essentially as Mrs. John Winthrop and hers did, in and before the open fireplace. By the end of the eighteenth century the cooking fireplace may have been out of sight in elegant mansions, but we may be sure that in the rear or in the cellar servants were stirring in iron pots and baking in brick ovens. The major changes in meal preparation came after the 1830s, when the iron cook stove with its fire enclosed was introduced. But it was not readily adopted until at least mid-century. After that, women cooked while standing upright, and the old fireplaces were sealed in the name of progress.

The Fireplace

Those old cooking fireplaces were gigantic. The fireplace in the 1720 addition at the Swett-Ilsey House in Newbury is reputed to be the largest in all the eastern settlements. It is 10'8'' wide, 5'4'' high, and 6' deep including the hearth. The typical first period Connecticut fireplace was over seven feet wide and nearly four feet high, and the lean-to fireplaces were even larger with openings over nine feet wide. The 1690 fireplace in the Buckingham House at Mystic Seaport takes eight-foot logs. The base of the chimney in the cellar of the Thomas Lee House (c. 1660) in Niantic, Connecticut, serving that typical salt-box house, is fourteen feet square, overwhelmingly impressive to view.

The very earliest fireplaces were made of wood and clay. Thus Deputy Governor Samuel Symonds wrote in his instructions to John Winthrop, Jr. in 1638 regarding construction of his one-room house in Ipswich, 'GI would have wood chimneys at each end, the frames of the chimneys to be stronger than ordinary, to bear good heavy load of clay for security against fire.'[7]

In general, after those very first years, fireplaces were made of fieldstone where it was available and of brick where the soil was clay-like for brick-making. Many houses near seaports had fireplaces made of bricks brought as ballast in ships from England. Handmade, sun-dried bricks were made before kilns were established, and binding mortar was made of clam or oyster shells and hay. The Colonel John Ashley House (1735) in Ashley Falls, Massachusetts, has a marble hearthstone, for there were large marble quarries in nearby Sheffield.

Fireplaces and hearths in the Massachusetts Bay towns north of Boston were of brick, for kilns were established very early there, and almost every town in Essex County had one.

Some fireplaces have built-in cubby holes, places to store things that had to be kept dry, such as tinder, in case some dreadful day the fire went out and another had to be started using flint stone. Gun-

Fireplace at Whipple House, 1670.

powder was also stored in the cubby hole, for if it were allowed to become damp, it would readily explode. The 1720 fireplace at the Swett-Ilsey House has such a cubby hole, and the Whitfield House has several holes used for salt as well as gunpowder.

Another sort of niche, called a smoke shelf or channel, is to be seen on the rear wall of the Whipple House fireplace in Ipswich, Massachusetts. It is a shallow depression starting about a foot above the base of the fireplace and continuing upward into the throat of the chimney. As an attempt to prevent smoking caused by down-draft in

15

the cavernous chimney, it was not too satisfactory. The smoke channel at the Buttolph-Williams House, a rear depression starting at the very base and extending upward, works well, and on a cool day visitors are treated to a fire and can see the smoke travelling up this channel.

The gigantic fireplace in the 1650 Ironmaster's House at Saugus, Massachusetts, has, not a depression, but a stone projection built into the brick side wall. This is the hob-nob, a seat right in the warmth of the yawning fireplace. Certainly in the evening with the day's cooking accomplished and the fire slowing down just before being banked for the night, this must have been a cozy place. If the night was clear, the person on the hob-nob could look right up the chimney and see the stars twinkling. On the other hand, if a storm was raging outside, rain or snow would spatter on the embers. The kitchen hob-nob at Saugus could by no stretch of the imagination have accommodated two people, yet the gossipy expression "she's been hob-nobbing with so-and-so" arose from such sharing of the seat in the fireplace.

Hob-nob in Ironmaster's kitchen/fireplace, 1650.

Fireback in parlor fireplace.

One of the products of the Saugus Iron Works was the fireback, a cast iron plate set against the rear wall to protect the bricks from the constant and intense heat of a fire that was seldom out. Some of the firebacks were very decorative with the owner's initials or coat-of-arms. The one in the parlor fireplace at the Ironmaster's house has a tulip design and the date 1650. The firebacks were sand-cast with the carved model of the design pressed into damp, hard-packed sand within an enclosing frame to form a "negative" onto which molten iron was poured and allowed to cool.

The north fireplace at the Henry Whitfield House is over ten feet across, and the chimney flue is so wide that it is divided in two by stonework to give structural support to the entire mass.[8] Inside this great fireplace is a bench to sit on for gazing at the stars or thawing out your bones. This fireplace, along with a somewhat smaller one at the south end of the Great Hall, presented a problem. One fire would draw from the other and cause it to go out. For preventing this and for cutting down the size of the Great Hall for more effective heating , the Whitfield builder provided a swing partition that let down from the ceiling and divided the Hall into two rooms.

Occasionally we find a cooking fireplace in the base of the chimney in the cellar, where the huge cooking jobs were done. The Judson House (1723) in Stratford, and the Leffingwell Inn (1675) in Norwich, Connecticut, have cellar kitchens. Abner Judson, son of David the builder, owned seven slaves at the time of his death in 1775. Tradition in Norwich says that slave auctions were held at the north door of the Leffingwell Inn. The slaves at these and other places probably worked in either kitchen, and the nature of the job more than the status of the cook determined which fireplace was used. At Leffingwell Inn the cellar hearth is provided with a gigantic spit, an iron cauldron, and an apparatus to mass produce candles, indicating the magnitude of the jobs performed there.

The upper reaches of the chimney could also be put to use, as shown in the Webb House attic where there is provision for smoking hams by using smoke that was escaping up the chimney anyway. The Deane House next door has its smoke oven in the chimney off the back bedroom on the second floor, and the Walsh House (1796) at Strawbery Banke, New Hampshire, has an attic smoke chamber. In these smoke ovens, or chambers, an iron rod extends across the width of the chimney with hooks to hold meat. The Crowinshield-Bentley House (1729) in Salem displays a Dutch crown meat hanger, a circular band of iron with several hooks on it.

So in kitchen, cellar or attic, the colonial chimney is a monument to versatility.

The Bake Oven

Excepting the earliest homes such as we see recreated at Plimoth, most seventeenth and eighteenth century New England homes had, as part of the kitchen fireplace, a bake oven, a brick-lined, round, domed enclosure often called the Bee Hive oven because of its shape, but never to be called a Dutch oven, which was something entirely different. The earliest bake ovens will be found in the rear wall of the fire-place either to the right or left of the center. Later variations placed the oven in one of the angled side walls of the fireplace, still sharing the flue with the fireplace. By the middle to later eighteenth century, the ovens were being built into one of the fireplace jambs facing the room, and such an oven had its own flue.

Stanley-Whitman fireplace showing bake oven and crane.

Certainly the housewife would have found this a safer and more convenient location than that where she had to reach over and around flames and burning logs. We can imagine her delight with her new home improvement.

With most of these on-the-jamb ovens there is a somewhat smaller recess just below the oven. This may have been for cooling ashes removed from the bake oven before transferring them to the wooden barrel to be saved for soap making, or it may have been used to store wood. Authorities differ on this point, and probably house-wives did, too.

The inner baking surface of the Bee Hive oven was from 26'' to 30'' in diameter, lined with a double row of bricks and with an opening kept as small as possible (14'' to 18'' wide and 10'' to 16'' tall) to minimize heat loss. The oven door was a wooden slab that was simply set in place. Some have a curved section of a tree limb attached for a handle, as at Harlow House (1677) in Plymouth, and some have a carved handle. By the time of the Revolution, the doors were of cast iron and were attached to the side by hinges. Some iron doors even had a little damper at the bottom for the draft, as at the Atiquarian House (1809) at Plymouth.

This is the oven from which issued the long-baked beans, the custards, the breads and cakes. By the late eighteenth century cooks began using it for meats. The method for using it was simple. First the housewife built a fire right in the oven to preheat the bricks. When they were hot enough, she raked out the ashes and inserted the food, then set the door in place to keep the heat in. The baking proceeded. That was a simple enough procedure, but it took a good deal of experience to know just how hot was hot enough. Dr. Reuben Woodward of Watertown, Connecticut, never trusted his wife to heat her own oven but always performed this service for her—a solicitude that nearly drove Mistress Woodward to distraction.[9]

The usual way to test the oven's temperature, was for the cook to insert her arm into the oven and start counting. Experience taught her how far she should be able to count before the intensity of the heat compelled her to withdraw her arm. If she had to withdraw before that number, it was too hot. If she could endure the heat beyond the number, it was not hot enough. A story is told of one pious woman who sang the Doxology through a specified number of times in preference to counting.

Now she quickly raked out the fire and ashes with either her iron hoe-like implement or an iron peel, a long-handled, flat shovel, and disposed of her ashes in the lower recess or in the fireplace. She might use a turkey wing or a hemlock bough to sweep the surface clean, or she might pour in a very thin, flour-and-water batter to bake quickly, which when removed carried the ash residue with it. The baked sheet of flour-and-water batter was called oven cake, and this is the cake that Marie Antoinette suggested the hungry peasants could eat. Cooks at Buckman Tavern on Lexington Green, where the Minute Men waited that April night, are said to have used this method.

20

Iron peel, also called a slice,
for placing food in bake oven.

With her oven hot enough and clean enough, the cook is assumed to have all her baking ready to go inside. She would take her wooden peel, which could reach to the rear of the oven, and with it place in the rear whatever required the longest baking time, then the rest of the baking according to diminishing baking times. Some cooks placed their breads on oak or grape or cabbage leaves to keep the bottoms clean, probably during summer baking when leaves were green.

Excellent bake ovens are to be seen at almost every New England house, but what shall we say about Thomas Griswold, who had three bake ovens built into his kitchen fireplace—that he loved his baked goods? Or that Mrs. Griswold was the best cook in Guilford and he supplied her with the best in equipment? At the Putnam Cottage (1690) in Greenwich, Connecticut, there are two bake ovens in the kitchen, one of them a pass-through oven with an opening in both the kitchen and the tavern room, which must have been very handy.

Fireplace Equipment

Around the fireplace stood a variety of handcrafted equipment. Bellows, tongs, fire forks and shovels hung near to help in fire building. Andirons were used in all but the poorest homes, where stones had to suffice for holding the logs. Andirons appear in inventories sometimes as *fire-dogs* and sometimes as *hand-irons*, and the larger ones equipped with hooks were called *spit dogs* or *cob irons*. *Creepers* were low irons placed between the great fire-dogs to help support the burning logs.

The spit dogs in the 1727 kitchen at the Crowninshield-Bentley House in Salem are tall with four pairs of hooks for holding the spit at various heights. At the top, a cup or cresset-like form holds a basin for the basting mixture. Some spit dogs have lower hooks for holding the drippings pan. This set does not, but there is an oblong grisset placed underneath to catch drippings.

Pots hung over the fire from hooks and trammels. In the 1600s, before the iron crane was in general use, its function was supplied by the lug, a heavy pole of green wood resting on a ledge built within each side of the fireplace high up. The lug pole had to be watched for signs of charring or brittleness so it could be replaced before the sad day when it broke, dumping utensils and dinner into the fire and possibly scalding cook or baby.

When the blacksmith arrived in the settlement, the swinging iron crane became a much sought-after improvement. Pot hooks came in long or short lengths, and trammels allowed for variations in height so pots and kettles could be hung high or low for slow or fast boiling. For flat cakes there were griddles that hung, some from a bail like a pot, and some, like the beauty at Buttolph-Williams, with a perfectly balanced half-circle rising to join the pot-hook.

The change from lug pole to iron crane was one of the two major improvements in the colonial cooking fireplace (the other was the moving of the bake oven to the jamb). However, according to one authority on the colonial fireplace, it appears that the brick or stonework of old existing chimneys was not disturbed for the sake of installing a new crane. Rather, the crane was installed when a new fireplace was being built with its bake oven forward as, for instance, at the time of a lean-to addition.[10] In some fireplaces, had the crane been added, the cook would have had some difficulty reaching her rear oven, but with the pole stretching entirely across her fireplace, she could build her fire and hang pots on the opposite side from the oven on baking days. The crane does appear, however, in some fireplaces that have rear bake-ovens like the Stanley-Whitman (1660) fireplace, which originally had its lug pole and now has a crane.

Teapot hanging from crane by means of a pot hook.

The lug pole in the 1650 fireplace at the Ironmaster's House in Saugus is made of iron—an interesting variation but quite logical since the iron works was just down the hill, and also in view of the fact that this was a "company house" whose headquarters were located in England, so no expense was spared!

The hearths in front of the fireplaces are generally wide, creating here another cooking surface. Toasting racks and roasting ovens could be set in front of the fire, and any number of little individual fires could be made of coals raked out in piles to serve three-legged spiders, pots, griddles, or flat-bottomed pots set on trivets.

The earliest arrangement for roasting a joint of meat was simply a rope suspended from the front facing of the fireplace with the joint securely skewered, possibly with a green stick, or stoutly tied at the lower end of the rope. A good twist sent it spinning so that all sides got a share of heat, and though the reverse action of the spin kept it turning for a while longer, constant attention had to be given to twist it as often as it came to rest. Frequent basting was also required to keep it from drying out.

Toasting rack and three-legged posnet (small pot).

"Spit-dog."

The next roasting spit was a rod resting on the hooks of the and-irons in front of the fire, one end of the rod bent to form a handle. It would be someone's hot job to rotate the rod so that the roast baked evenly. A great improvement over that method was the clockwork jack, a system of wheels and weights that mechanically kept the spit in motion. These were not automatic for the entire roasting time, but were rewound and started again sometimes as often as every three minutes. The Silas Deane House (1766) in Wethersfield has one with shiny brass parts, a handsome piece of equipment that was found during restoration of the house in a jumble of tarnished and grease-encrusted pieces which, when cleaned and assembled, became part of the attachment of the jack and the pride of the Deane House curator.

And there were other spits. A standing iron rod with hooks to hold small birds was called in Rhode Island the Bob White spit. Another low tin rack with hooks arranged for something to lay horizontally was used for fish or roasting ears of corn.

The tin roasting oven was perhaps the great invention of its day, for it was closed on the side away from the fire, thus retaining and reflecting heat back onto the roast, which rotated on a spit within the tin enclosure. The back of the oven had a door that lifted so that basting could be accomplished at a somewhat more comfortable distance from the flames of the fire. Rotating the spit by hand was a job that usually fell to the children. Pictures and newspaper advertisements from Philadelphia support the use of dogs running a treadmill to turn

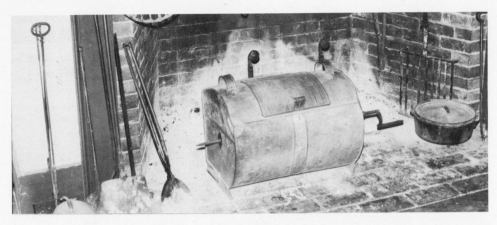

Tin roasting oven, showing the door through which
the roast could be basted and the handle for turning the spit.

the spit, but that does not seem to have been so common a method in
New England.

A supply of iron skewers hung near the fireplace for holding meat
on the spit, and in several cases the maker of the wrought iron skewer
holder lavished a special bit of attention to make it a decorative as
well as utilitarian piece. The holder in Joshua Hempsted's 1678
kitchen in New London is fashioned in a heart shape, and the long-
handled flesh fork hanging next to it has three tines, the center one

Roasting oven turned around to show the spit.

the point of a heart set between the others. This simple artistic embellishment in such a common article as a fork or a skewer holder says so much about the craftsman who made them, about his ability to put beauty into the utilitarian, his good taste in the restraint. Was he a bridegroom crafting his bride's first household needs?

Spit apparatus at Ironmaster's House. Wheel at top and weight on hearth are part of the jack. Note skewers and skewer-holder.

The Dutch oven was not the Bee Hive oven but a heavy iron pot with a flanged lid. Bread and biscuits could be baked in this pot, which was set over its own pile of hot coals on the hearth with more coals heaped onto the lid, thus providing heat top and bottom. Timing was important, both at the beginning and at the end. The embers had to be of slow-burning wood and glowing, not flaming, before starting the bake. And cook had to have a second sense about the amount of time required for baking, for peeking in was next to impossible. First, to remove the hot cover she would use awkward, long handled tongs, and furthermore, for just a look she risked tilting the cover so the ashes and embers would sift into her precious bake. So she left it "till done," then pushed off the ash and remaining embers, probably also using her turkey wing to sweep the cover clean. Only then did she remove the hot cover. It now appears through recent research at Plimoth Plantation that the Dutch oven was not in use during the earliest years of settlement but was an innovation that came along about mid-seventeenth century.[11]

Dutch oven.

In the well-polished, do-not-touch kitchens which we visit to get a glimpse of colonial living, we frequently find the museum's entire collection of cooking utensils arrayed in and in front of the fireplace. This cannot be avoided where the purpose is to show the various items and explain their use, but usually any given museum fireplace has more pots, pans and tools than the average colonial housewife owned or would use on any given day. Furthermore, she would not keep them all on the hearth for fear of tripping over them and falling into the fire. She generally had a water kettle going at all times and a pot over the fire, or a griddle, or the spit in operation, or a Dutch oven, but not all of them for the same meal. Inventories taken at the death of the head of household give us precise information as to the earthly goods in the home. Since these were taken by appraisers walking through the house and barns, it is fairly easy to imagine entering the kitchen with them and taking count of what was there in the way of cooking and dining equipment.

William Averill of Ipswich left a very modest estate valued in 1652 at £50. There were nine Averills, and their meals were prepared with "one iron pott, one brass pott, one frying pan, four pewter platters, one flagon, one iron kettle, one brass kettle, one copper, one brass pan and some other small things" appraised at £2-17-0."[12]

And while poking about the Averill home and hearth we might take time to distinguish between his iron "pott" and his iron kettle. Pots had a cover and bulging sides that grew narrower at the top, but kettles were always open and grew wider at the top.[13] Pots tended to be no larger than twelve gallons. Kettles frequently reached sizes of thirty gallons for operations like scalding the hog, boiling down sap, making apple butter, washing clothes, making soap—all big jobs that often were done outside where the iron cauldron or kettle hung on a tripod over an open fire.

John Higley, a runaway apprentice to a London glover, came to Simsbury, Connecticut, in 1684, and soon established himself as a leading citizen rising through the ranks to Captain of the Traine Band. He died in 1714 possessed of an estate valued at over £605, a great deal of this amount in land and livestock. Yet we can be certain his household goods were at least somewhat above the average. When the appraisers arrived in the kitchen they found that the Higleys owned:

    one great cupboard and one small cupboard
    one brass kettle and one kettle more
    one small brass kettle and skillet
    one iron kettle and two small skillets
    brass mortar and pestle
    one iron pot and one iron pot more and hooks

one great pewter platter and one pewter basin
one small pewter platter and three old plates
one pewter flagon and four pewter cups
one quart pot and one pewter tankard
one copper cup and one poringer
three candlesticks and a funnel
one stone jug and one knot dish and three spoons
two wooden bowls—other wooden dishes
one pail, trenchers, and tub
glass bottles and vials
one hour glass—salt cellar & a wooden can
one pitobere and table linen
two tramels, one pair of tongs and slice
cob irons—flax combs—four jacks
five chairs—two more chairs.

Captain Higley bequeathed one-third of his estate to his wife and divided the remainder among his 15 children, the eldest son getting a double share.

When the Captain's son, Brewster (not the eldest), died a half century later in 1760, his goods and holdings were valued at £936, and his kitchen furnishings were:

3 bibles and sundry other books (which must have been in
   the kitchen for they come between the livestock and
   the cooking equipment)
iron pot, tramel, fire tongs, fire slice
hand irons, brass kettle
two iron kettles
brass mortar
funnel
table, buttermould
small brass kettle
frying pan
iron skillet
six pewter platers
eleven pewter plates, seven pewter basons

two pewter porrengers, beaker, old tankerd
quart cup, pint cup, old pewter, tin kulender, tin pan
saucepan, skimmer, tonel, coffepot, jackknife
seven knives & forks, lanthorn, milk bowls
spice morter, two woden platters knot dish & skimer
seven trenchers, four milk bowls, water pail, churn.

After this the appraisers go to the looms, bedsteads and bed linen, where, among sheets and towels are:

six napkins, two table cloaths, one napkin, pitcher, flask, and four glass bottles

When Brewster's son, Ensign Brewster, died in 1794, after the Revolution and almost into the new century, he left an estate of £946. He had a pork barrel, sider barrel, one meat barrel and one tub, another sider barrel, which would all appear to have been together in a room perhaps off the kitchen. Then follow:

one pewter quart cup
one pint do [for ditto]
one puter plater and one do
one puter bason
one puter tea pot, five old puter plates
one pint basin, one tin funel
two knifes and forks
one iron pot
one iron kittle, grid iron
one iron tramel, one pair old hand irons
one old pare do, one spade
one slice, one pair tongs, one old do
one chest of drawers, low do
one long table, one small do
one old chest, one trunk
three best chears, three old do
one stool, one pair large stilyard, small do.

Elsewhere in the house Ensing Brewster had one case and bottles, one frying pan, an old brass kittle, and a looking glass, an old chest, old barrel, one basket, another, and one wood two quart bottle.[14]

These inventories of three generations in the same family, from the same town, show very little change in possessions over the course of a century. Ensign Brewster had no trenchers, but it should also be noted that he has no plates. Possibly by 1794, the old wooden trenchers were not considered worth enough to merit listing. Then, too, woodenware made by hand within the family was generally excluded from inventories;[15] hence, only a few mugs or trenchers ever show up. Ensign Brewster did have a tea pot, a new item for the Higleys, but his father had owned a coffee pot.

Other Kitchen Furnishings

The furnishings of a kitchen attest to the varied activities that went on there. We would consider a table essential, and except in the very earliest settlement there would have been one, perhaps a trestle table or a stretcher table, or a hutch table whose surface could be turned back revealing an extra seat. There would be stools and a form (bench) and a chair.

A chest was more common than a table in the earliest years and provided storage as well as a working surface until a table could be acquired. There are many beautiful chests in New England's historic houses, often with the tulip or sunflower design so popular in the Connecticut Valley, often with facades decorated with two-dimensional, carved motifs or with applied moldings and split spindles. On the chest might lay the carved Bible box, protecting the leather-bound Book of Books, which every family had and which was the only book that most families had.

A cupboard or hanging shelves or a "dresser" would provide keeping space for the porringers and plates, trenchers, spoons, bottles, drinking horns, charger, in short, the family supply of tableware

Hanging shelf with tankard, calabash, and jug.

whether of wood or pewter. There was very little silver in the early
days.

A bench or a board laid across two saw horses or a narrow table
held the cheese and sausage making equipment in season, or the candle molds in candlemaking season. We must make room also for the
kettle of wax at the fire and bring ladder-back chairs to lay candle rods
across. In dye season, take care not to tip over the blue indigo kettle.
The other dyes from wild plants were made and used out-of-doors, but
indigo remained by the hearth in colder weather.

There's the churn, later in the Pilgrim Century, with its up and
down motion at the Thomas Lee House (1660) in Niantic and the Putnam Cottage. It was made of tin for the Stanley-Whitman kitchen in
the late eighteenth century, but some Yankee ingenuity is displayed
at the Thomas Griswold House (1735) in Guilford, where the churn
has cog wheels so lucky dame or maid simply turned a handle.

Taking up more space than can easily be spared in this busy room
is the wool wheel, the huge one where a spinster might walk 20 miles
in a day back and forth in the graceful motion of spinning wool. Atten-
dant with this are baskets of fleece to be carded by granddame or child
sitting at the fireside in the evening, as well as baskets of carded wool
waiting to go on the spindle. The flax wheel, being smaller, did not
have to remain in the way of traffic when not in use.

By the fireplace stood the settle in cold weather, its seat too narrow for comfort but its high back keeping cold drafts off while the front of a body roasted in the radiance of the fire. At the Buttolph-Williams House and at the Mission House the settle backs are gracefully curved.

Sometimes there's a tiny settle with a hole in the seat, which was baby's potty chair. At the Hempsted House is a baby's go-cart or walker, and at the Crowninshield-Bentley House is a baby-tender consisting of a hoop to go around the toddler's middle, attached to a pole going from ceiling to floor which allowed the young walker to go round and round well away from the fire. The Buttolph-Williams House has twin high chairs, and playpens are shown at the Bates-Scofield House (1736) in Darien, the Mission House, and the Keeler Tavern (1772) in Ridgefield, Connecticut. And of course, the cradle rocked near the warmth of the fire.

In the majority of restorations there are no signs of a sink. Perhaps a wooden tub on a bench was all the poor lady had. But at the Silas Deane House there is one sink worth special mention. A granite

Sink at the Harlow House, Plymouth. Drain at far end
can be seen beaneath wooden hatch.

slab with a depression in it plus a trough to the side for drainage was found in the cellar during restoration. Imagine the thrill of the antiquarians when they discovered that it fit perfectly into an alcove in the kitchen, and a plugged-up hole in the wall was found to align exactly with the trough! Water was drained directly to the hollyhocks or whatever grew just outside.

The Harlow House in Plymouth also has a stone slab sink, sort of oval in shape. Such sinks were made of sandstone in the Connecticut Valley, of gneiss in the hills, of slate and of marble in areas where they were found. Some sinks drained by gravity through a hole into a pail beneath instead of outside. Near the sink would hang a bundle of twigs, the Horse-tail Rush or "scouring rush" (*Equisetum hyemale*), the colonial S.O.S. pad, as well as a container of sand for scrubbing iron pots. At the Silas Deane house, conveniently sized sections of worn-out patchwork quilts hang for dish towels.

Hanging from the beams in late summer were bunches of drying herbs. As pretty as it may look to have them hanging from the lintel over the fireplace, the colonial housewife probably hung them from beams away from the fire. At Plimoth dried, salted fish hang across one wall, and onions, too. In the corners of the room might be two sacks or boxes of Indian corn, rye, dried pease or beans. In autumn apple and pumpkin slices strung on linen threads would be hanging to dry.

A Betty lamp might hang from a beam near the fireplace, and tucked behind a beam somewhere was the almanac for the year. There was a birch broom in the corner, and in the evening chips fell from a new one being made by a boy in the family.

And we haven't mentioned the ladles and skimmers, the firepan for taking to the neighbor's when the fire went out in those days before matches, and the footstove of perforated metal holding coals for warming the feet at "meeting," the lantern with horn sides, and pails with bails and pails without bails but with ears through which a pole was laid for carrying, and the wooden yoke to make carrying two pails easier, and the leather bucket, required firefighting equipment, the spice box and the spice mill or mortar, the butter paddles and butter molds, the powdering-trough which was a tub containing a pickle for salting meat, and the keeler or tub for holding milk for cream to rise on it. And somewhere in the early days, was the tree

Corn morter made from hollow tree trunk with
a pestle made from a limb.

trunk hollowed out to make a corn-grinding mortar, its pestle a tree
limb with its end rounded off. There's one at the Buttolph-Williams
House, another at Hempsted, and one with a crook making a natural
handle at Stanley-Whitman.

All these furnishings picture for us the activity in the kitchen: the
boiling, baking, roasting—the churning, candlemaking, carding, spinning, dyeing—whittling, knitting, patching, and mending—the active
babies, the family gathered for high noon sustenance or evening devo-
tions. Though not all activities were in motion on a given day, it was,
nevertheless, a busy room and leisure came in the guise of a sit-down
job.

Still we cherish a vision of tranquility reigning in these homes. Is
it an invention of ours, or do we sense it through diary entries like
Abigail Foote's for June 9, 1775: "I did housework in the forenoon and
I wove in the afternoon and went with Ella a-strawberrying."[16] On
another June day in 1784 Dothe Stone of Litchfield, a young woman
who would be married in a few months to Younglove Cutler of Water-

town, recorded in her journal, ''I have just had time to milk the cow since I returned from picking strawberries. . . . A pleasanter night I never saw. . . . The moon shines pale and pleasant in at the south door. . . . Mama is singing to her dear little Polly in the middle room. She has a fine soft voice.''[17]

Can it be that these women were attuned to a different sense of time, that they labored at feeding and clothing their families not in order to get the job done to get on with an errand or a trip to the orthodontist? The colonial housewife was not straining to get away. Her labors became her purpose in life. In providing her loved ones' daily nourishment, she was participating in God's plan for His faithful elect. To the Puritan, work was holy. Thus she found harmony where we would find monotony.

The motions of spinning at the tall wool wheel, lifting the arm, touching the wheel, stepping back and walking forward, feeding the wool to the wheel, gave the spinning woman a stately grace unmatched in modern woman, and as she put herself into the rhythm of her daily and seasonal pursuits, her spirit, too, reflected the grace and harmony of the spheres.

Cheese press, Whipple House.

DINING CUSTOMS

Besides his traditions in house building, the New World settler also brought with him long-standing habits of dining, and his stomach told him in New England as in Old when mealtime had arrived and what sort of response it expected from him. The English husbandman of the sixteenth and seventeeth centuries dined at high noon and supped at seven or eight.[18] Breakfast was taken after the fire had been replenished and the porridge cooked, and while Goodwife was thus occupied, Goodman took care of his stock. Then the night's fast was broken.

The historians at Plimoth Plantation have depicted a medival life-style in their recreation of life there from 1620 to 1627. Their best research indicates that the antecedent life of these Pilgrims was rural-yeoman, the style depicted in the Dutch paintings of the 1500s. Unfortunately, England had no school of interior domestic painting, but the Low Countries and England were not so unlike, and many of the American Pilgrims had sojourned in Holland. Thus, these pictures may be taken as fair indicators. They verify many things found in inventories, archeological digs and bequests to succeeding generations: cooking furnishings were meagre and dining was somewhat casual, with people seated perhaps on a bench with a trencher between them, perhaps at a table formed by a board on a barrel, or at a chest. In the simplest cottages there might not be any table, at least not for everyone in the house, and the lap sufficed.

Though casual as to seating arrangements, diners did not consume their meal casually. In fact, "the act of breaking bread together was in the secular sense 'almost a sacramental matter.'"[19] The mealtime atmosphere was relaxed and happy and unhurried. After the hard work of securing and preparing, one would not take lightly the gift of food provided for him. Writing in 1557 (and reprinted over and over), Thomas Tusser advised the English huswife,

> At bed and at board, howsoever befall,
> Whatever God Sendeth, be merry withall.[20]

At Harvard College in the seventeenth century, breakfast was taken after the 5 a.m. prayers. It consisted of bread and beer, called the "morning Bever," and was picked up at the buttery hatch to be consumed in the student's room.[21]

In the fashionable homes of England in the 1700's, breakfast was later, dinner was taken about two o'clock and lasted through the afternoon, and a cold supper was eaten just prior to bedtime. Undoubtedly the style-conscious in America dined similarly. Samuel Sewall noted in his Diary in July 1687, that he supped at the Grayhound Tavern and "came home between 10 and 11, Brave Moonshine."[22] And on June 30, 1704, "after Dinner, about 3 p.m." he went to view an execution.[23] In New York the new President breakfasted at 7:30 or 8:00, dined at 3:00 and supped at 8:00, while outside the cities dinner was at 2:00, and this remained the practice until the mid-1800's.[24] Writing in 1811, Timothy Dwight reported that fashionable people in New England "breakfast late, and dine from three to four."[25]

Samuel Goodrich wrote of his boyhood in Ridgefield, Connecticut during the last decade of the eighteenth century, "In most families, the first exercise of the morning was reading the Bible, followed by a prayer, at which all were assembled, including the servants and helpers of the kitchen and farm. Then came the breakfast. . . . The day began early: breakfast was had at six in summer and seven in winter; dinner at noon—the work people in the fields being called to their meals by a conch-shell, usually winded by some kitchen Triton. The echoing of this noon-tide horn, from farm to farm, and over hill and dale, was a species of music which even rivaled the popular melody of drum and fife. Tea—the evening meal, usually took place about sundown.''[26] That everyone in Ridgefield called farmhands to dinner at about the same time, noon, gives credence to the opinion that in the rural parts the "farmers' nooning" did indeed take place at noon despite the fashionable two or three o'clock city dinner that lasted all afternoon.

A city meal was described by Henry Wansey, travelling through America in 1794. At his accommodations in Boston he was served in what we would call family style, with all the dishes of the main course put on the table at once. He writes, "At two o'clock dinner was announced, and we were shown into a room where we found a long table covered with dishes, and plates for twenty persons. We were served with salmon, veal, beef, mutton, fowl, ham, roots, puddings, etc. etc. Each man had his pint of Madeira before him, and for this our breakfast, tea, supper and bed, we paid five shillings currency. . . . In half an hour after the cloth was removed every person had quitted table, to go to their several occupations and employments . . . for the Americans know the value of time too well to waste it at table.''[27] This meal was served at an inn, or tavern, frequented by working people of Boston, perhaps shopkeepers, perhaps lawyers, perhaps craftsmen—at any rate, working people who took their dinner at two o'clock and did not linger, at least not more than half an hour after the cloth was removed, when wine and fruit would have been placed on the bare table.

We see then that dining times in both the seventeenth and eighteenth centuries were determined by social class. The yeoman-farmer of the seventeenth century dined at noon just as the post-Revolutionary rural farmers. Pilgrim Century Bostonian Samuel Sewall and the "fashionable people" observed by Timoth Dwight more than a hundred years later dined in mid-afternoon. As for Wansey's 2:00 p.m. fellow diners, though they had "occupations and employments" they dined in a manner that would indicate they were of the rising middle class and possibly quite urbane.

The Menu

The common breakfast, especially in the first century of settlement, was salt meat and bean porridge, says Connecticut historian George Clark.[28] Hasty Pudding, Joel Barlow, the Connecticut poet, called it. By the late eighteenth century breakfast for Lyman Beecher consisted of rye bread, fresh butter, buckwheat cakes and pie.[29] Samuel Goodrich's breakfast about the same time was "a substantial meal, always including hot viands, with vegetables, apple-sauce, pickles, mustard, horseradish, and various other condiments,"[30] and for John Adams breakfast was always preceded by a "large tankard of hard cider."[31]

The noon meal was the heartiest of the day, with salt pork or a boiled corned beef dinner or a meat pie, perhaps a roast of venison or other game or fowl from the roasting spit, or a planked fish. Vegetables were boiled, for in their natural state they were considered "unwholesome," and usually vegetables and meat (unless spitted) were boiled all together. Such a meal was preceded by the pudding. After a life of service to his country in the White House and in foreign countries, John Adams retired to Quincy and had his Indian Pudding before Sunday dinner for the rest of the his days.[32] The Beechers also considered this a Sunday tradition. Lyman writes, "We dined on salt pork, vegetables, pies; corned beef also, and always, on Sunday, a boiled Indian pudding."[33]

Supper, or tea, was usually cold and always light with cornmeal cakes or samp or hominy in the first American century. In 1811, Timothy Dwight wrote, "Supper in most parts of the country is like the breakfast, except that it is made up partially of preserved fruits, different kinds of cakes, pies, tarts, etc. The meats used at breakfast and supper are generally intended to be dainties."[34] Writing of the meals in the homes of Gloucester fishermen, Samuel Eliot Morison also notes that the supper menu was the same as breakfast (tea or coffee, rye and injun bread, salt or fresh fish, plus, at supper, cheese, cakes, gingerbread, or pie."[35]

Homely customs change slowly. The writer's family lived in the same part of Connecticut from the first generation of settlers to her own, and Grandmother, nearing 100 in the 1930s and with no men farmers left at home, still cooked a hot meal at noon and had to the end of her life tea and toast and applesauce for supper.

Serving the Meals

So much of what we see and read about table settings and foods of that encompassing "colonial" America period is really eighteenth, even late eighteenth, century. The customs and foods of the Pilgrim century were quite different from those of the Patriots of '76. After all, a century and a half had intervened.

In most of the historical houses we visit around New England, it is evident that life has progressed to a "solid sufficiency," and the table is made to appear as if a simple country meal were about to be served. At the Parson Capen House (1683) is a trestle table of grand size, 10' long, 2' wide, and 3' high, set with wooden and pewter ware. The Tristram Coffin House in Newbury has an old and a new kitchen, and in the new (1725) kitchen is a Queen Anne gate leg table made of tiger maple scrubbed nearly white through the years. This table is set with pewter plates and two-tined forks and knives.

At the head of such a table sat the head of the family in possibly the home's only chair. It might be a wainscot chair brought from England, its solid oak panels elaborately carved, or a Brewster or Carver chair with beautifully turned spindles at its back, the Brewster having them also below the rush seat. Whatever the style, it was the place of honor and everyone else sat on joined stools or a form, a bench without a back, and in some homes children and servants stood. Today we recognize this practice when we name the head of a committee the chairperson and give him/her the seat at the head of the table. When we speak of the endowed "chair" at a college, we also perpetuate the sense of honor attached to being seated in the chair.

With the family gathered about the board, the housewife brought food to the table in a large wooden or pewter charger and set it in the center. The husband asked God's blessing on the food before them and at the conclusion of the meal he would offer thanks for what God had supplied, whether it was a haunch of venison or the meagre allotment of corn in the famine days. The food was then ladled from the charger, which was similar to our deep platters, onto trenchers, or possibly, if the family had the barest modicum of earthly things they all dipped their spoons, or sippets of bread, directly into the charger and so shared the meal.

Madam Sarah Kemble Knight, who travelled from Boston to New York by horseback in 1704 (an unheard-of accomplishment for a woman in her day), noted that in Connecticut "they generally lived very well and comfortably in their families. But too indulgent (especially the farmers) to their slaves: suffering too great familiarity from them, permitting them to sit at the table and eat with them . . . and into the dish goes" everybody's hand.[36]

The trencher was a 10" to 12" square or rectangular block of wood as thick as 3" or 4" with a bowl carved into it to make a dish. In the Pilgrim century a person shared a trencher with another. Husband and wife, two or more children, and perhaps the whole family would eat from one, depending on the family's circumstance or preference. Alice Morse Earle tells of a duke and duchess living in England in 1750, who all their lives had eaten from one trencher as a sign of their devotion and unity. She also tells of a Connecticut deacon who acquired a lathe and made a trencher for each member of his family only to be severely criticized for such ostentation.[37] Possibly this is the same man of whom the story is told that he was denied election to the office of deacon because of his extreme display in having a single trencher for each of his children.[38]

It also seems to have been a custom that when a young man and woman shared a trencher at one or the other's home they were considered engaged. There is an old expression, seldom used anymore but worthy of remembrance, describing a man of hearty appetite as "a good trencherman." There is a splendid trencher at the Thomas Lee House and a small, oval-shaped one at the Ironmaster's House.

Trencher and wooden cooking spoon.

The term *trencher* is sometimes applied to lathe-turned plates. As soon as there was a cooper in the settlement, he easily found employment making plates when demand for his barrels was slack. Wooden plates were also available from merchants. Knife marks show on both sides of many old plates indicating that the tradition of a "dinner side and a pie side" is perhaps valid, although no contemporary references to this economical practice have been found.

That plates were valued and scarce possessions is shown at the Hyland House in Guilford, where sometime, long ago a wooden plate broke in two, and someone raised by the philosophy of "Make it, Mend it, Make it do or do without" laced it together with linen thread which still holds.

The best collection of wooden or treenware to be seen anywhere in New England is at the Buttolph-Williams House in Wethersfield. Here is probably every wooden utensil of colonial times from beautiful bowls made of the burls occasionally found on maple trees, to ladles, mugs and mortars large and small. It is not typical of the aver-

Woodenware at Stanley-Whitman House. The lamp is a "rush-lamp."

age New England family's stock of treenware but the wide variety of wooden utensils nevertheless offers a feast for the eye.

So, with the charger on the table and the trencher before them, the family ate, using spoons and knives. Forks did not come into general use until after 1700, although Governor Winthrop had received one as a gift in 1633 that he kept in its case to show as a curiosity. The fork was introduced to England from Italy by Thomas Coryat after his 1608 European tour of the continent. A member of the royal household, Coryat would have had an intense interest in such style as dining with a fork, and he not only brought back one for his own use, but he also wrote and published an account of his journey in which he described how the Italians "do always at meals use a little forke when they cut their meat."[39] The first dining forks were two-tined; three-tined came late in the eighteenth century.

In 1719 in the western frontier settlement of Deerfield, John Sheldon died possessing four knives and three forks and certainly had not just acquired them, so the fashion had caught on in distant settlements as well as in Boston.[40] We get a further insight into habits from a study of Deerfield inventories where it is revealed that "the number of napkins decreases as knives and forks become more common."[41] Before forks, the well-bred English were using their fingers for chunky and solid foods, spoons for the rest.

The early knife was a pointed utensil, the point being used to anchor down the chunk of meat while the fingers broke off or pulled off a daintier piece. Knives were made of steel with wooden or bone handles, and there are knives made entirely of wood that were rather broad and with a sharpened edge. One is shown at the Hawthorne birthplace in Salem.

Spoons were made of horn, wood or pewter, with horn, perhaps, the most commonly used. A lengthy process of soaking and boiling and pressing was required to turn an ox horn into a spoon for the table, but the end result was a quite attractive, tannish, rather translucent implement (Peeled very thin after boiling, horn became transparent and hence was also used to cover the printed paper on children's horn-

Pewterware, Stanley-Whitman House.

books.) Every horn spoon I have seen at the historic houses has been oval-shaped in the bowl, which would date them eighteenth century, for seventeenth century spoons had round bowls.

Cider and beer were the common beverage, one or the other present at every meal, and the tankard or mug was passed from hand to hand around the table for all to drink. Tankards are tall mugs with handles and hinged tops. Some were made of pewter, some wood, and in the case of wooden ones the handle and vessel were likely to be carved all from one piece of wood.

One further piece appeared on the table by tradition, and that was the standing salt. It might be the family heirloom, brought from England and very elegant, or it might be a humble piece of treenware carved by the fireside, but it was essential both for flavoring and for its social purpose. The place one was assigned at table in relation to the salt revealed his relative importance in the group. If you sat "above the salt," that is, at the host's end of the table, you could consider yourself esteemed. If you were "below the salt," the message was equally clear. Thus, husband and wife sat side-by-side, not at opposite ends of the table.

At the close of the meal a basket, called the voider, was passed and everyone placed his spoon and trencher and knife, if he had one, in it for cleaning, and another meal was done. Thanks again to the merciful God who had provided and blessed.

Equipage of the Table

From inventories of estates among the first generation of Pilgrims, R.B. Bailey concludes that a large number of napkins was required at these forkless tables (as already cited from the Deerfield study). Bailey also finds table or "board-cloths" were used. Most tables were covered not just with one but with two cloths, one atop the other. The decorative tablecloth was a Turkey carpet, and when the term *carpet* frequently appears in inventories it is the table, not the floor-covering, that is indicated. These carpets were English products with a knotted pile made in imitation of rugs from the Near East, or "Turkey." There is evidence in some Dutch domestic paintings to suggest that white linen cloths were spread over the Turkey carpet for dining. Whichever way, it was on the white linen that the dinner was set.

Of course the earliest settlers brought their utensils from home. We need not imagine that first settlers immediately went about making the treenware we so much admire. There were pewter platters,

Turkey carpet, Ironmaster's House.

cups, flaggons, salts and other utensils named in first generation inventories that Bailey studied, and little ships like the *Mayflower* were very soon sailing back and forth across the Atlantic bringing articles from the home country and taking back native products. One reason colonization was encouraged was to provide a market for English goods.

As for what colonists should bring with them, broadsides were circulated in England and the Rev. Francis Higginson wrote a prospectus setting forth the wonders of the country in an attempt to sell it to new immigrants. Evidently satisfied that it would have the desired effect, he listed on the last page of the second edition the necessary things to bring in the way of clothing, arms, tools, spices and food-stuffs for a year. Under the heading Household Implements he lists:

1 Iron pot	1 Spit
1 Kettell	Wooden platers
1 Frying pan	Dishes
1 Gridiron	Spoones
2 Skellets	Trenchers[42]

With these supplies in the trunk, immigrants could confidently face the realities of settlement.

As we move along through the 1600s from the first settlement, we find more craftsmen and tradesmen and goods arriving, so that Englishmen in the plantations (the "planted" colonies) of New England, ever anxious to live as they had back home, increased their supply of earthly goods. Subsequent settlers also had the advantage of bringing more goods with them, so life was by no means a make-shift, camp-out affair.

Pewter and treenware were used side-by-side in New English homes throughout the colonial period. Lyman Beecher (born 1775) wrote in his *Autobiography*, "We had wooden trenchers first, then pewter, and finally earthenware,"[43] and Connecticut pewterer Thomas Danforth Boardman wrote in his, "From the Landing of the Pilgrims to the Peace of the revolution Most all, if not all, used pewter plaits and platters, cups, and porringers imported from London and made up of the old worn out."[44] Students at Harvard ate from both wooden and pewter utensils.[45]

Every historic house open to the public displays some pewter, with excellent pieces to be seen in Connecticut at the Bush-Holley House (1685) in Cos Cob, the Judson House in Stratford, and the Coffin and Swett-Ilsey Houses in Newbury, the latter having a magnificently large pewter charger.

Unfortunately, you will often hear about a great amount of lead poisoning suffered by those who ate from pewter. It just is not so. The pewter pieces from England were made under the strict regulation of the Worshipful Company of Pewterers, one of the strongest of the guilds, which could confiscate sub-standard pewter and have the maker fined and/or imprisoned. Although the Guild's powers were not enforceable in America, early craftsmen here had learned their trade under its aegis in England. Furthermore, colonial people were quite aware of the danger. In 1678 for example, Bostonians warned that "care may be taken that all wares made of pewter or silver, whether brought to the countrie or made here and exposed to sale may be of ye just alloy."[46]

Fine pewter was entirely free from lead while the lowest grade could contain up to 40 per cent lead for use in wine measures and chamber pots. Ordinary dishes and plates, ale mugs and porringers were made of the middle quality metal containing about 5 per cent lead. According to Charles F. Montgomery, curator of the pewter at Winterthur, "Lead-adulterated pewter was the exception rather than the rule."[47]

In 1635, there arrived in Massachusetts young Richard Graves, who had completed his apprenticeship as a pewterer in England. Most of the business for Graves and the three other pewterers who were in Boston as early as 1640, was reworking badly dented articles into new ones. This reworkable quality of pewter indeed made it handy, even though it did dent easily.

Joshua Hempsted of New London recorded in his diary for Nov. 25, 1743, "Set out for Norwich . . . I caryed up 7 lb and 15 oz old Pewter . . . to Sandford to work up for me."[48] Eight days later it was ready, and on "Dec. 3 . . . I brot home a New Pewter plate and 3 plates made with my Pewter 6 lb and 6 oz."[49] Possibly Sandford was entitled to the difference of 1 lb. 9 oz. of his customers' old metal for his own stock, to enable him to have pewter to sell to the public.

The *Connecticut Courant* for July 20, 1767, carried the following advertisement:

Henshaw and Hamlen, Braziers and Pewterers,
Hereby inform the Public, that they have lately set up their Business, at the Shop of the Widow Hooker, near the North-Meeting-House, in Hartford; where they make, and have for Sale, Brass Kettles, Tea-Kettles, Coffee-Potts, Quart and Point Potts, Basons, Plates, Dishes, Platters, Porringers, etc. on the most reasonable Terms, for Cash, Country Produce, old Pewter, Brass, or Old Copper.

N.B. They mend all Sorts of Copper, Pewter, and Brass Wares.[50]

Since pewter was easily melted down by heat, many homes could cast or re-cast their own spoons, and we frequently find a mold on view at the historic houses. The Judson House has one. It was not a difficult fireside task. We remember that women and girls in Litchfield melted down the lead from the statue of King George III and cast bullets to return to his Redcoated soldiers, and some patriots made household pewter into bullets at their home hearths.

Pewter tablewares consisted of plates, saucers, "open salts, porringers, mugs, tankards, and basins (called breakfast bowls, if small, and wash basins, if large)."[51] Montgomery found that covered tankards were favored in New York, but that "Connecticut Yankees, like New Englanders in general, seem to have preferred to drink from open mugs."[52] Babies had their pewter sucking bottles and little children their pap spoons.

Our colonial housewives took pride in their pewter and kept it gleaming. This is unfortunately not the condition in which we see it in most historic houses, where its dinginess may be attributed to a laudable attempt not to harm the artifact by incorrect cleaning. In museums, such as New Haven Colony and Essex Institute however,

Pewter charger and mugs, Harlow House.

the pewter is polished and bright. Montgomery gives a safe cleaning method in his work, *A History of American Pewter.*

Earthenware came along after treen and pewter, at least in the Beecher household. Since it is easily broken, it is not likely settlers would have used precious space trying to bring such wares with them. The appearance of a few pieces in Plimoth inventories leads Bailey to wonder if early trading with Indians might not have provided the Pilgrims with earthen dishes.[53] In 1635 Phillip Dunker, potter, arrived at Charlestown, Massachusetts aboard the *Abigail*, the same ship that brought Richard Graves, pewterer. Other potters arrived shortly thereafter, and clay works became common in the towns of the Bay Colony.

The type of pottery coming from the early pot works was redware, made from the same red New England clay that was used for bricks. All earthenware is opaque, whereas china is translucent, and all earthenware is porous and must be glazed. Powdered lead, sand, sometimes ground glass and water were all ground and mixed together to make a glaze to apply to the air-dried earthenware. Then during firing the glaze turned shiny and transparent. A large earthen pot, glazed inside but not out, was intended not for Saturday night beans but for butter or lard, with the inside glaze necessary to overcome the porosity on the food side, and the unglazed outside to keep the contents cool through the effect of cellar or dairy dampness. Such a pot is to be seen at the Josiah Day House (1754) in West Springfield.

To apply decoration, the potter used a substance called slip, a clay of contrasting color diluted with water and trailed in a thin stream around the earthen piece from a quill or a slip cup, which had a hollow pipe. After further sun-drying, the glaze was applied over everything and the piece fired. This decorated and glazed ware is called slipware. Whereas ordinary red, glazed earthenware may date from the mid-1600s, slipware dates from 1725 and after.[54]

Many houses have a few pieces of earthenware, but by far the most extensive and absolutely handsome collections are in the butteries at the Hyland House and the Ashley House.

Delftware pieces add a touch of color to the treen and pewter settings at many houses. The Crowninshield-Bentley dining table is set with Dutch and English delft, for example. The Buttolph-Williams House has a mug celebrating the Union of Scotland and England,

Staffordshire and pewterware, Whipple House.

which dates it nicely at 1603. Delft tiles are on the fireplace jambs at the Shaw Mansion, but in the bedroom instead of the cooking fireplace.

Delftware is a plain clay pottery with a thick white glaze into which colors of the decoration were painted before the piece was fired.[55] The Dutch brought this ware to New England in trade for fish and furs as early as the 1630's at Plymouth, and shortly thereafter at Connecticut River ports and Portsmouth, New Hampshire. The

English made delft-type ware after 1671, the date of the pot works at Lambeth. English delft shows a rosy tint through the white glaze and the blue decoration is a bit grayish.[56]

Americans were anxious to buy the beautiful imported ware. Josiah Wedgwood himself said the colonies in 1765 were a "market for the more costly wares made at the British potteries."[57] These are the pieces that were treasured and handed down to succeeding generations and that show up today in museums and historic houses. The English and Dutch delft, the Leedsware, the Staffordshire, Wedgwood, and Whiedon survived. Too much of the ordinary earthenware found its way to the trash pit.

One other ware was found on colonial tables after 1750. This was chinaware, arriving from the Orient by way of England because of trade restrictions. It was then very expensive, but after the war American trade took over and in 1784 the first American ship arrived in Canton Harbor to be followed soon by enterprising merchant traders of Salem, Boston and other American ports. Soon every shop in New England had Canton ware or Chinese export porcelain along with teas, textiles, and other exotics of the China trade.

Ranging from the rude trencher to the delicacy of Chinese porcelain, colonial tableware presents a variety of styles and materials. Each historic house shows the type most appropriate to its particular time and station. The best way to see the entire range is to visit a museum complex such as Historic Deerfield, Webb-Deane-Stevens in Wethersfield, or the Essex Institute in Salem.

Life Style

If we exclude religious matters, it is probably at the dining table that cultural differences strike the most personal chords of our being, and if we were actually to sit down to dine with a seventeenth-century family we would assuredly suffer shock. Not only would our superior knowledge of germs make us shrink from the common tankard as it passed from lip to lip, but also the shared trencher and the hands dipping into the charger for a chunk of meat would disturb our sensitivities. Actually, early America of the 1600s was more medieval than modern or even Renaissance, and here is the crux of our problem.

The medieval man or woman viewed all aspects of life as communal. All family activities in the one-room house were shared, communal activities, not because the architecture dictated it, but because it was considered the natural way of life. Meals were communal. Theology was communal (the Puritan emphasized the sharing aspect of the Lord's Supper rather than the sacrificial aspect). Philosophy was communal (the Mayflower Compact stresses the community, not the individual: We "covenant and combine ourselves together in a civil body politic . . . and promise due submission to the general good. . . ."}.

With the Renaissance came the idea of individualism by which we organize our lives: the individual cup and plate, the individual bedroom and individual rights as, for example, expressed in the Declaration of Independence.

This notion of communal vs. individual life-style belongs to Prof. James Deetz, recently professor of anthropology at Brown University, who developed it from discoveries made in his archeological digs around New England and especially at Plimoth, where he was Assistant Director. Most intriguing is his analysis of bones found at home trash sites: those recovered from sites dating prior to 1700 show that meat was hacked into convenient size by the use of an axe. With this kind of meat cutting, the cook had no choice but to boil her meat in the pot until it fell from the bones, or to roast it until well enough done so that the family could pull it from the bones using knife and fingers in a communal serving.

On the other hand, bones found in post-1700 trash pits had been cut with saws. Individual servings were becoming the accepted style, for chops and steaks are possible only when saws are used.[58]

The communal meal is at one extreme of our colonial period. At the other extreme is the late eighteenth-century aristocratic dinner.

Settings

For the merchants who were amassing fortunes from trade and for the "codfish aristocracy" whose fortunes were made on the fishing banks, the tabletop reflected a new life-style more vividly, perhaps, than any other aspect of the home. Now the Boston or Portsmouth or New Haven lady wanted to set out a table in the best and latest English fashion. Near the end of the century she had cookbooks to tell her exactly how to do it, offering sample bills of fare for two- and three-course dinners, even presenting a diagram of how the dishes should be set on the table.

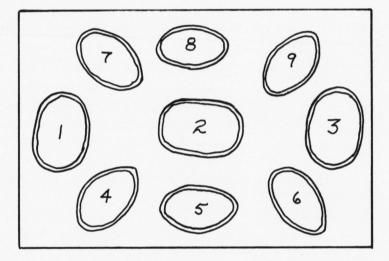

A standard British work, Susanna Carter's *The Frugal Housewife, or complete woman cook*, was reprinted in Boston in 1772 and in Philadelphia in 1796. Mrs. Carter recommended a two-course dinner, each course consisting of nine dishes to be arranged on the table in the following manner.[59]

She provided a sample menu for each month of the year, suggesting for February:[60]

First Course

1. Dish of Fish.
2. Pease Soup.
3. Fillet of Veal.
4. Chickens.
5. French Pye.

6. Beef Collops.
7. Ham.
8. Rump of Beef à la Daube.
9. Marrow Pudding.

Second Course

1. Wild Fowls.
2. Epergne.
3. Hare.
4. Cardoons.
5. Scalloped Oysters.

6. Tartlets.
7. Stewed Pippins.
8. Ragout Mellé.
9. Artichoke Bottoms.

All the dishes of the first course were set out on the table, which was covered with two white linen cloths. When the dishes of the first course were removed the top cloth was also removed. The same procedure was followed for the second course, so that dessert was served on the bare table. This would have been the style observed at the Boston home of Peter Faneuil when "he and his friends sat down to two courses, the first of four different kinds each of soup, fish, and meat dishes and 12 lighter dishes of fish or meat. The second course featured four roasts of birds and rabbits, 12 dishes of vegetables, jellies, and four sweetmeats and biscuits."[61]

John Adams, riding circuit in 1774, reported to Abigail back home in Braintree about his dinner in Falmouth, District of Maine, "and a very genteel dinner we had. Salt fish and all its apparatus, roast chicken, bacon, peas, as fine a salad as ever was made, and a rich meat pie. Tarts and custards, etc., good wine and as good punch as ever you made."[62] Such meals always impressed New Englander John Adams and he never failed to be amazed at the "sinful display" of foods, which he obviously enjoyed immensely in homes where he was dined in Philadelphia. At Mr. Miers Fisher's he was served "ducks, hams, chickens, beef, pig, tarts, creams, custards, jellies, foods, trifles, floating islands, beer, porter, punch, wine—and a long etc."[63]

That was Philadelphia. But Portsmouth, New Hampshire was equally fashionable with the royal governor setting a royal style. In Wethersfield, worldly Silas Deane set a fashionable table, and next door, Mrs. Webb, who reacted to news that George Washington was to be her house guest by having the front chamber papered, surely lavished as great attention on her dinner menus, though to our great loss, no accounts exist about the meals she served on that occasion. A few years before, John Adams had been entertained at the Webb's "most genteely," as he noted, "with punch, wine, and coffee."[64]

But Timothy Dwight, commenting on the fashionable dinner, thought that "the dining table is loaded with a much greater variety of dishes than good sense will justify."[65] And back home, not only in the Adams house in Braintree, but in the homes of all honest farmers and craftsmen of New England, dinner was still a simple meal with pudding and cider, a roasted joint or a one-pot stew served in the homely treen or pewter ware. This was the everyday fare of the average rural and small-town New Englander. This was life in the typical saltbox house.

THE FOODS

We hear of want and famine in the first years of settlement and wonder how that can be with the ocean's plenty in front and the forest's full game basket behind the tiny villages. The reason lies with grain. Before he left home for the New World, the average English yeoman "was accustomed to a diet that gave him almost six thousand calories a day,"[66] supplied not by fish, flesh and sallets, but by bread, porridge, butter, cheese and ale. In Plimoth the first year's crop of peas failed and the barley was only "indifferent good,"[67] according to William Bradford. It was Indian corn that saved the day and provided enough for each surviving Pilgrim to be allotted two pounds of corn per day following the 1621 harvest, the year of the first Thanksgiving.

In 1623, the *Ann* arrived with 60 more mouths to be fed. They brought no foodstuffs of their own, and everyone at Plimoth dipped into their stores to share, so no one actually starved. But all were hungry that winter.

In general, though, colonists had "good living."[68] They testified to this themselves in the accounts they sent back to England. These accounts were intended to attract more settlers to emigrate, and as "travel brochures" they are enthusiastic (though occasionally in their exuberance they are unreliable, as in the report of lions on Cape Ann[69]). But we can take them as indications of New England's summer plenty.

In 1630 Rev. Francis Higginson wrote, "This Countrey aboundeth naturally with store of Roots of great variety and good to eat. Our Turnips, Parsnips and Carrots are here both bitter and sweeter than is ordinarily to be found in England. Here are also store of Pumpions, Cowcombers, and other things of that nature which I know not. . . . The Aboundance of Sea Fish are almost beyond believing . . . such aboundance of Makerils that it would astonish one to behold, likewise Cod-Fish . . . and abundance of Lobsters, and the least Boy in the Plantation may both catch and eat what he will of them. For my owne part I was soone cloyed with them, they were so great, and fat, and lussious. I have seene some myself that have weighed 16 pound."[70]

William Wood's account in *New England's Prospect* (1635), subtitled "A true, lively, and experimentall description" of New England, tells us, "The ground affoards very good kitchin Gardens . . . and whatsoever growes well in England, growes as well there, many things being better and larger: there is likewise growing all manner of Hearbes for meate, and medicine, and that not onely in planted Gardens, but in the Woods, without either the art or the helpe of man. . . . There is likewise Strawberries in abundance, verrie large ones, some being two inches about; one may gather halfe a bushell in a forenoone."[71]

Roger Clap's testimony was written as his memoirs rather than as advertising, and with the advantage of hindsight in 1731 he tells us of life in the 1630s in Dorchester and Windsor, "In those days God did cause his people to trust him, and to be contented with mean things. It was not accounted a strange thing in those days to drink water, and to et samp or homine without butter or milk. Indeed it would have been a strange thing to see a piece of roast beef, mutton, or veal; though it was not long before there was roast goat. After the first winter, we were very healthy, tho some of us had no great store of corn. The Indians did sometimes bring corn, and truck with us for clothing and knives; and once I had a peck of corn or thereabouts, for a little puppy-dog. . . . If our provisions be better now than it was then, let us not . . . forget the Lord our God."[72]

In addition to this cornucopia of native products and those cultivated from seeds brought from home, colonists had almost from the beginning a steady supply of imported goods. Every ship that arrived carried goods to be exchanged for native products, for this was where the ship owner made his profit, and as soon as the colonist could turn his attention from the priority of establishing his colony, he was, building ships and gathering stuffs to enter the lucrative trade cycle. Every schoolchild is familiar with the routine and route: take American lumber and furs to England and trade for English products to bring home, or take American products to the West Indies and trade for sugar and molasses. The first molasses arrived in Boston port in the late 1600s and was an immediate hit as a sweetener and raw material for "that Devil rum." Then it was to Africa with the rum and back with the black man. "Molasses for rum for slaves."[73] It was trade that made the colonies prosperous and instigated the move for independence.

All kinds of products flowed in. In 1732 John Merrett, grocer, offered "At the Three Sugar Loaves and Cannister near the Town-House, Boston . . . Cocoa, Chocolate, Tea, Bohea and Green, Coffee raw and roasted, all sorts of loaf, powder and Muscovado sugar, Sugar-Candy brown and white, candy'd Citron, Pepper, Pimienta or Alspice, white Pepper, red Pepper, Cinnamon, Cloves, Mace, Nutmegs, Ginger race and powder, Raisins, Currants, Almonds sweet and bitter, Prunes, Figgs, Rice, ground Rice, Pearl Barley, Sago, Starch, Hair-Powder . . . Corriander & Carraway Seeds . . . fine Florence Oyl, Vinegar, Capers, Olives, Anchovies, and fine English pickled Wallnuts. . . . The said John Merrett has lately Imported fresh Supplys of all sorts."[74]

In 1768 John Crosby, "Lemon Trader near the Sign of the Lime," offered "Fresh Lemmons at 12 s. per dozen."[75]

That same year, people in the western Connecticut town of Woodbury read in the Connecticut Courant: "Tomlinson and Huntington of Woodbury have just imported in the Ship New York, Capt. Lawrence, from London, and have for Sale . . . Allspice, Cinnamon, Cloves, Mace, Nutmegs, Pepper, Loaf Sugar, Wines, French Brandy, etc."[76]

Lathrop and Smith of Hartford offered Books, Painters Colors "together with Loaf Sugar of various qualities, Best Claret and Madeira wine—West India Rum by the Hogshead, Barrel, or Gallon—Ginger—Pepper—Allspice and other Spices—Choice Indigo—Rice—French Barley—Oatmeal—Raisins—Figs—Tamarinds—with a Variety of other Articles."[77]

The ships also brought people with skills who settled here and offered the products of their skills to the public. "John Ingram, the Original Flower of Mustard Maker, from Lisbon, now living at the house of Mrs. Townsend, near Oliver's Dock, Boston, Prepares

Flower of Mustard to such Perfection, by a Method unknown to any Person but himself, that it retains its Strength, Flavour and Colour Seven Years, being mix'd with hot or cold water, in a Minute's Time it makes the strongest Mustard ever eat, not in the least Bitter, yet of a delicate and delightful Flavour, and gives a most surprizing grateful Taste to Beef, Pork, Lamb, Fish, Sallad, or other Sauces. . . ."[78]

The colonial housewife, that new American woman, took then, these foodstuffs and at her hearth created the dishes that in turn created a tradition of "good hearty fare." Some of her ways of doing this are revealed in the recipes that follow.

Corn

Any discussion of colonial foods must begin with corn, the grain that made possible the settlement of America from Plymouth straight across the continent. When we visit our historic houses, we should be able to see in our mind's eye the field of corn stalks out the window, greening, tasseling, or drying according to the season.

Indeed, from the first discovery by the Pilgrim scouting party of the Indian's cache of seed corn on Cape Cod a few days before their arrival in Plymouth, this New World maize was the life-saving food of the infant settlements. It was the manna feeding these pilgrims so they could get along with their mission of establishing God's Kingdom in New England. Every day the grain bubbled in the pot or baked in the oven of New England's huge fireplaces. One may wonder at the ingenuity of our pioneer mothers in varying the manner in which they prepared this grain which was, after all, new and strange to the first immigrants. Just as Squanto taught the Pilgrims how to plant corn (in hills) and how to fertilize it (three herrings in each hill), he went on to teach them some Indian methods of preparation which yielded succotash, roasted ears, Nokake, even Johnny Cake and popped corn. The English women took it from there and substituted cornmeal for English wheat, which did not grow well in New England, and so made their Indian Pudding, Hasty Pudding, Bannock, and Corn Chowder.

Hasty Pudding: Joel Barlow, one of the Hartford wits of the late eighteenth century, treated the homely dish of Hasty Pudding with all the grandiloquence of an ancient epic:

"I sing the sweets I know, the charms I feel,
My morning incense, and my evening meal,
The sweets of Hasty Pudding. Come, dear bowl,
Glide o'er my palate, and inspire my soul . . .
Thy name is Hasty-Pudding! thus our sires
Were wont to greet thee fuming from the fires;
And while they argu'd in thy just defence
With logic clear, they thus explained the sense:—
'In haste the boiling cauldron, o'er the blaze,
Receives and cooks the ready-powder'd maize;
In haste 'tis serv'd, and then in equal haste,
With cooling milk, we make the sweet repast.
No carving to be done, no knife to grate
The tender ear, and wound the stony plate;
But the smooth spoon, just fitted to the lip,
And taught with art the yielding mass to dip,
By frequent journeys to the bowl well stor'd,
Performs the hasty honors of the board.'
A name, a sound to every Yankee dear,
But most to me, whose heart and palate chaste
Preserve my pure hereditary taste. . .
Thy constellation ruled my natal morn,
And all my bones were made of Indian corn.
Delicious grain! whatever form it take,
To toast or boil, to smother or to bake,
In every dish 'tis welcome still to me,
But most, my Hasty-Pudding, most in thee."[79]

In 1795, a group of Harvard students formed a literary and patriotic group called "The Hasty Pudding Club." "On 'Pudding' nights, when the bell tolled for the scanty evening commons, two members might be seen bearing on a pole an iron pot of steaming Hasty Pudding from some near-by goodwife's kitchen to a member's room, where the brethren supped on that simple but filling fare."[80]

63

To make *Hasty Pudding*

Mix 1/2 cup of yellow cornmeal with 1 cup of cold water. Boil 2 cups of water, add 1/2 tsp. of salt, and then add the cornmeal-water mixture, stirring constantly. Continue to cook and stir for about 15 minutes. If preferred, you may cook it in a double boiler for 30 minutes to eliminate the stirring. Serve hot with cold milk or butter or molasses, or sugar and nutmeg.

The traditional way to eat Hasty Pudding is to have a "puddle" of butter melting in an "excavation" in the center of the pudding in your bowl. You then take a spoonful of pudding from the edge of the bowl, where it is somewhat cooler, dip it into the butter, and make the "journey" to the mouth.

Indian Pudding: An Indian Pudding is not the same as Hasty Pudding, as even a brief glance at the recipes will show. This pudding can serve as a dessert, though John Adams began his dinner with it.

2 cups milk	1/2 tsp. salt
1/4 cup yellow cornmeal	1/2 tsp. cinnamon
1/2 cup molasses	1/2 tsp. nutmeg
1 egg	1/4 tsp. ginger
1 Tbsp. butter	1/4 c. raisins (optional)

an additional 1/2 cup cold milk

Scald 1 3/4 cup milk; use other 1/4 c. milk to mix with cornmeal. Add cornmeal and milk mixture to scalded milk. Cook in top of double boiler for 15 minutes, then add rest of ingredients, and pour into a greased baking dish. Bake in slow oven, no more than 300 degrees F. for 15 minutes. At this point pour the extra 1/2 cup cold milk over it, but DO NOT STIR. Bake 1 to 1 1/2 hours longer, till bubbles appear on top. Serve warm with cream or hard sauce or vanilla ice cream.

The first cookbook by an American author to be published in the United States was *American Cookery* by Amelia Simmons. In her first edition, 1796, Mrs. Simmons offered three recipes for *"A Nice Indian Pudding."*

#1: "3 pints scalded milk, 7 spoons fine Indian meal, stir well together while hot, let stand till cooled; add 7 eggs, half pound raisins, 4 ounces butter, spice and sugar, bake one and half hours."

In #2 she adds molasses and uses only 2 eggs.

With #3 she directs the method for cooking, "Put into a strong cloth, brass or bell metal vessel, stone or earthen pot, secure from wet and boil 12 hours."

Butter mold, funnel, and pitchers, all treenware.

Johnny Cake: The origin of the name *Johnny Cake* is obscure, but most historians think it is a corruption of *Journey Cake* and that the original was a sort of flat cake that could be baked on a board slanted before an open fire and could be mixed up easily by a person on a journey or working a great distance from the home. They were also made in the home and are no different from Bannock in mixing or baking, though Bannock was originally made from oatmeal instead of cornmeal.

> Boil water, pour it over "a sufficient quantity of cornmeal" and let it stand until the meal swells to about double (about 10 minutes). Thin with boiling water to desired consistency, and fry by spoonsful on a hot griddle in butter as you would pancakes.

This, however, is a far cry from what the electric range generations think of when they think "Johnny Cake." The modern version is cake-like. A good recipe for this *Johnny Cake* is:

> Sift together in a bowl:
> 1 cup yellow cornmeal
> 1 cup sifted flour
> 1/4 cup sugar
> 1/2 tsp. salt
> 4 tsp. baking powder
> Add: 1/4 cup soft shortening
> Mix together separately:
>   1 egg and 1 cup sweet milk
> Add the liquid ingredients to the dry ingredients and shortening, and beat with egg beater until *just* mixed. Bake in a greased 8" square pan, at 425 degrees F, for 20 minutes. Serve hot.

If you have at your dinner table a Rhode Islander and a New Englander from any of the other five states you had best not serve Johnny Cake, for it will start a controversy beside which religion and politics would look pale. Rhode Islanders use white, not yellow corn meal, and have done so from the start. And while Connecticut had Joel

Barlow to rave over Hasty Pudding, Rhode Island had "Shepherd Tom" Hazard to write an encomium on the subject of Rhode Island Jonny Cake.

"Nowhere else on the globe," stated Tom, could real, white Indian meal be found, "a food originally designed and set apart by the gods exclusively for their own delectation." In Tom's youth (he was born in 1797) his grandfather had "in his kitchen an old cook by the name of Phyllis, originally from Senegambia, or Guinea, who probably made as good a jonnycake . . . as was ever made outside of heaven . . . (Phyllis) always insisted on having white Narragansett corn, ground at . . . Hammond's Mill, which is situated on the site of the elder Gilbert Stuart's snuff mill. . . . Nor could Phyllis be induced . . . to touch meal ground at any other mill."[81]

Once Phyllis got her meal, and once Tom got on with his story, for he delighted in digression, she:

> "proceeded to bolt it through her finest sieve, reserving the first teacupful that fell for the especial purpose of powdering fish before their being fried . . . she continued with the same sieve to bolt about one-half of what remained for her jonny-cakes. . . . She proceeded to carefully knead it in a wooden tray, having first scalded it with boiling water, and added sufficient fluid, sometimes new milk, at other times pure water, to make it of a proper consistency. It was then placed on the jonny-cake board about three-quarter of an inch in thickness, and well dressed on the surface with rich, sweet cream to keep it from blistering when placed before the fire. The red oak jonny-cake board was always in the middle portion of a flour barrel from five to six inches wide. This was considered an indispensable requisite in the baking of a good jonny-cake. . . . The cake was next placed upright on the hearth before a bright, green hardwood fire. This kind of fire was indispensable also. And so too was the heart-shaped flat-iron that supported it. . . . When the jonny-cake was sufficiently done on the first side, a knife was passed between it and the board, and it was dextrously turned and anointed, as before, with sweet, golden-tinged cream, previous to being placed again before the fire."[82]

While Shepherd Tom grudgingly allowed that "a decent jonny-cake can be baked on a coal stove, though by no means equal to the old-time genuine article,"[82] most of us will have to be content with the modern version, lacking as we do the red oak board, the heart-shaped flatiron and the green, hardwood fire—not to mention Phyllis's talent.

Rye n' Injun Bread: Bread made with corn meal alone dries out quickly, so to prevent staleness rye flour was added to make Rye 'n Injun Bread, which Shepherd Tom spelled Rhineinjun, adding that it is "vulgarly called nowadays rye and Indian bread." A modern version of *Rye 'n Injun* is:

Blend 1 cup cornmeal, 1 cup rye flour, 1 cup white flour together. Scald 1 cup milk, and allow it to cool. Add 1 cup water with 1/2 a yeast cake in it. Add flour mixture, 3 Tbsp. sugar, 1 tsp. salt and stir well. Then knead well. Let rise until top cracks, cut down, and knead again. Shape into loaves. Place in greased bread pans and allow to rise till double in bulk. Bake at 350 degrees F for about 1 hour.

In his digression on Rhineinjun bread, Shepherd Tom explains two methods of baking. "One way was to fill two large iron basins with the kneaded dough, and late in the evening, when the logs in the kitchen were well burned down, to clear a place in the middle of the fire to the hearth and place the two basins of bread, the one on top of the other, so as to inclose their contents, and press them into one loaf. The whole was then carefully covered with hot ashes with coals on top, and left until morning." This method produced a bread with a "thick, soft sweet crust."[83]

"Another was to place a number of loaves in iron basins in a log-heated and well-tempered brick oven. . .into which a cup of water was also placed to make the crust soft. The oven door was then closed and plastered up. When the door of the oven was opened in the morning it was customary to raise one or two windows in the kitchen, the fragrance from the bread being so enrapturing as sometimes to affect persons whose nerves were not very strong."[83] Consider yourself duly warned!

Boston Brown Bread: Boston Brown Bread is a close kin to Rye n' In-jun, but it is steamed, not baked, and is sweeter. Here is a workable version of *Boston Brown Bread*:

Combine: 1 cup yellow corn meal, 1 cup rye flour,
        1 cup wheat flour (graham), 3/4 tsp.
        baking soda, and 1 tsp. salt.
Combine: in a separate bowl: 2 cups sour milk, 3/4 cup
        molasses, and 1 cup chopped raisins.
Add the liquid to the dry ingredients. Pour the batter into a buttered mold, filling it 2/3 full, no more. Steam for 3 1/2 hours.

Method for Steaming

Place your molds on a rack in a kettle large enough so a cover will fit tightly when molds are in it. Have water enough already boiling so that it will come up halfway on the molds. Place molds, tightly covered themselves, on the racks. Cover the kettle and keep water boiling for the time specified. Water may be added as the level goes down, but always add water that is already boiling, otherwise your bread will be heavy.

Succotash: Indians taught the Pilgrims to make Succotash, but it was a far different concoction from the Succotash we make today. A Plymouth Colony recipe calls for:

1 quart pea beans
6 pounds corned beef
5 pounds fowl
5 quarts hulled corn (see below)
1 medium turnip
5 medium potatoes (if desired)

Soak beans overnight, then cook and mash. This makes the thickening. Boil beef and fowl until tender, and save liquor. Cut up turnip and potatoes and cook in the liquor. Cut the beef and fowl into 1/2 inch cubes. Combine all ingredients and let boil together for about 1 hour. Stir frequently to keep from sticking. Let cool, always uncovered. Stir occasionally to keep from souring. Serve in soup plates. This is better the second and third day.

To make the Hulled Corn: Soak overnight 1 quart dry yellow corn in two quarts of water in which you have dissolved 2 Tbsp. soda. Boil in same water next morning for 3 hours, adding water as needed. Drain, wash, rub off hulls by hand. Boil again in fresh water. Drain again. Boil 4 hours in fresh water with the salt added. It is now ready to eat with milk or butter. To use in Succotash, you would figure backwards so its last hour of boiling was in the pot with the Succotash ingredients.

A modern Succotash, the one on which your writer was reared, is:

Take about a dozen ears of fresh corn-on-the-cob, husked and with silks carefully removed. Using a wooden chopping bowl, because it is shallow and easy for the next step, cut the kernels off and scrape downward to get all the milk.

Shell your fresh lima beans, about 2 quarts will do, and boil them until tender in water with a good tsp. of salt and a few pieces of salt pork. When they are tender (the water should be almost gone and if it is not then pour off some), add the cut corn, and cook about 5 to 10 minutes until the corn is cooked, but not tough. Be careful not to boil hard or it will stick down.

Add a little heavy cream and a good piece of butter, and serve in a bowl as a side dish at dinner.

Mother always decided it had a few too many beans, so the next day we would add some corn. She then decided it was a little too heavy on the corn side, so we picked, shelled and boiled up more beans and added them. This was just about right. We couldn't keep this process up too long, for even with modern refrigeration succotash will sour, but it was fun for a few days to carry on so.

Corn Pudding: Once the colony had cows enough, corn was used in puddings, which were a favorite dish of the English. Corn pudding resembles a baked custard with corn added.

Beat one egg. Add 1 cup milk, 1/2 tsp. salt, 1/2 tsp. sugar, 1/2 Tbsp. butter, a few grains of pepper, and 1 cup corn scraped from cob (or use canned corn). Turn into a buttered baking dish, or individual custard cups. Set in shallow pan of hot water. Bake at 350 degrees F for about 45 minutes or until center is firm.

Beans and Peas

Pease Porridge: There were other foods to stick to the ribs and see a person through a hard day's work of settling a colony. We remember one only as a nursery rhyme, but Bean, or Pease, Porridge was a hearty thick soup on olden times:

Pease porridge hot, pease porridge cold
Pease porridge in the pot nine days old,
Some like it hot, some like it cold,
Some like it in the pot, nine days old.

Like many soups and stews, this one improves with age, hence reference to the nine days. It was often frozen with a loop of string in it so that it could be hung in the cold buttery or woodshed and in this manner also could be carried into the woods or on a journey to supply the midday meal.

Pease, or Bean, Porridge

1-1/2 cups dried beans or pease
a 3 lb. to 4 lb. piece of lean corned beef
1/3 cup cornmeal

> Soak beans overnight in cold water. In the morning drain. Cook beef till it falls apart. Remove from water. Cool and shred it. Cook beans till tender in beef water. Add cornmeal, cook and stir till thickened. Then add beef and taste before seasoning.

Baked Beans: If there is a national dish in this country, it has to be Baked Beans. We can try to regionalize them by naming them "Boston" Baked Beans, but they're still universal, from Maine to Long Island Sound and from Sutter's Creek, where they're called Pork and Beans, to Manhattan and the Rockies where they're adulterated by the addition of tomatoes and steamed rather than baked. They achieved their first popularity because of the strict Puritan regard for the Sabbath, to keep it holy. The beans could bake all day Saturday and be ready to feed the family on the Sabbath without anyone having to profane the day by labor. They could be carried to meeting to be eaten cold between morning and afternoon services.

By the early 1800s, bakers in larger towns were performing the job of baking great quantities of beans in their customers' own bean pots and delivering them to homes, along with a loaf of steamed brown bread, in time for Saturday night supper. Here's one you can do at home:

> Pick over and wash one pound of beans. California pea beans are favored. Put them in a kettle and cover with fresh water and let stand overnight. Next morning drain them, cover with fresh water, set on the fire and bring them slowly to a boil. Cook gently until the skins wrinkle and crack when exposed to air—take one up on a spoon and blow on it to test.

> Now rinse with cold water and place them in a two-quart earthenware bean pot. Pour boiling water over a good-sized piece of salt pork, scrape the rind until white, score it in strips and press into the top of the beans.

> Now make the sauce: To 3/4 tsp. dry mustard, 2 tsp. salt, 1/8 tsp. ginger, 2 Tbsp. white sugar, and 1/4 cup molasses, add 1 1/2 cups boiling water and mix well. Pour this over the beans.

Cover the pot and bake 9 hours in a slow oven. Add 1/2 cup more water every half hour or so, but never to cover the beans—just so bubbles can be seen on top.

Pumpkins

In the cornfield grew pumpkins, making frugal use of the cleared land. Their October orange surely delighted the colonists' eyes as it does ours. If we may judge from one anonymous colonist, pumpkins may have been just a little too abundant on the colonial menu. A six-stanza poem called "Our Forefathers' Song" was dictated *memoriter* in 1785 by a lady then 96 years old. It may have been composed during the 1630s by Edward Johnson. Stanza IV goes:

"If fresh meat be wanting to fill up our dish,
We have carrots and turnips as much as we wish;
And is there a mind for a delicate dish
We repair to the clam banks, and there we catch fish.
Instead of pottage and puddings and custards and pies,
Our pumpkins and parsnips are common supplies;
We have pumpkins at morning and pumpkins at noon;
If it was [sic] not for pumpkins we should be undone.[84]

The lack of pottage and custards lamented in the poem was shortly to be remedied by some innovative cook when she departed from the English idea of pie as a meat-filled pastry and instead filled her crust with pumpkin stewed in the Indian fashion. Then, with inspiration she added an English custard, some West Indian molasses, and so invented pumpkin pie.

Sift together: 1 cup sugar, 1 Tbsp. cornstarch, 1/2 tsp. each salt, cinnamon, ginger, nutmeg. Mix with 1 3/4 cups stewed pumpkin wor 1 #2 can). Add 2 eggs beaten, 1 1/2 Tbsp. melted butter, and 1/8 cup molasses, and 1 1/2 cups warmed milk. Pour into pastry lined pie tin (9") and bake in 425 degrees F oven about 40 minutes. Serve with cold cider.

However, before that inspired day there was a simple and useful way to prepare a *Baked Pumpkin*:

Cut a hole at the stem end of a pumpkin, reach in and clean out seeds and tissue. Replace end and bake. When done, fill with new milk and eat contents with a spoon. Keep shell, dry it, and use it to hold yarn or cloth bits.

John Josselyn reported in his *New England's Rarities*, 1671, on ''An Ancient New England Standing Dish'':

''The Housewives manner is to slice them when ripe and cut them into Dice, and so fill a pot with them of two or three Gallons and stew them upon a gentle fire the whole day. And as they sink they fill again with fresh Pompions not putting any liquor to them and when it is stir'd enough it will look like bak'd Apples, this Dish putting Butter to it and a little Vinegar with some Spice as Ginger which makes it tart like an Apple, and so serve it up to be eaten with fish or flesh.''[85]

Piggin, Whipple House.

This sounds like the "sause" which Madam Knight was served with "Rost Beef" in Stonington on her trip in 1704. She also was offered a "Pumpkin and Indian mixt Bred" at Stratford which "had such an Aspect" she declined.[86] Few, however, will decline a modern *Pumpkin Bread*:

3 eggs
1 one-pound can solid pack pumpkin
3/4 c. cooking oil
1/2 c. water
2-1/2 c, sifted flour
2-1/4 c. sugar
1-1/2 tsp. baking soda
1-1/4 tsp. salt
3/4 tsp. nutmeg
3/4 tsp. cinnamon
1/2 c. raisins, chopped a bit
1/2 c. chopped walnuts or pecans

Beat together in large bowl the 3 eggs, pumpkin, oil, and water. Sift together the dry ingredients and add them to pumpkin mixture, folding them in. Then fold in the raisins and nuts.

Bake in two greased and floured loaf pans at 350 degrees F for about 1-1/2 hours. Cool on rack for five minutes, then remove from pans to complete cooling.

Other Vegetables

There were other vegetables which grew in plenty, like sparrow grass, or asparagus, turnips, parsnips, carrots, cucumbers and squash, whose Indian name gave early writers a bit of trouble. Josselyn referred to squotersquoshes, Roger Williams wrote askutasquashes, and

Wood's variation was isquokersquashes. Josselyn described it as "a kind of Mellon, or rather Gourd, for they oftentimes degenerate into Gourds; some of these are green, some yellow, some longish like a Gourd, others round like an Apple, all of them pleasant food boyled and buttered, and season'd with Spice."[87]

Potatoes

Far from being the staple they later became, potatoes were eyed suspiciously, and people feared they would shorten life, or worse, act as an aphrodisiac (the same property frequently attributed to tomatoes). Writing in 1790, Samuel Deane acknowledged that potatoes were classed by botanists as "poisonous plants" but added, "If they were eaten raw, perhaps they would be found to be very unwholesome. But . . . the action of fire renders them very wholesome, and nourishing to man and beast."[88]

Deane also dates its introduction to this country for us. "It is more than half a century since this root found its way to this country and within twenty-five years they have been much cultivated."[88] This would lend credence to the tradition that the Irish settlers to Londonderry, New Hampshire, introduced the potato to America in 1719.[89]

The potato was described in 1803 as "the most valuable root . . . that nature has produced, a North American native, introduced to Europe by Sir Walter Raleigh, who cultivated it on his estate in Ireland,"[90] which would explain how the Londonderry settlers became familiar with it in the beginning.

A Hadley farmer is said to have harvested eight bushels of them in 1763, a crop considered too large since "if a man ate them every day he could not live beyond seven years."[91] But by the time Mrs. Simmons brought out her cookbook in 1796, she could recommend the potato roasted, boiled, as stuffing for turkey or wild fowl, as a pie, and for making a good starch. Mrs. Tallmadge of Litchfield made a *Potato Pudding*:

Take one pound of mashed potatoes, three quarters of a pound of butter, as much sugar, 7 eggs, a Gill of Brandy, a Gill of Rose Water, a Gill of Cream. Work the butter and potatoes together. The sugar and eggs must be beat to a froth, and then mix it all together.

Roasted potatoes offer us the simplest adaptation of colonial cooking with only a fire in the fireplace required. With no Bee hive oven or crane, or even a Dutch oven we can still bake potatoes as our ancestors did by wrapping the potato in wet leaves and covering it with hot ashes. It takes from half to a full hour to bake depending on the size of potato.

The potatoes that were imported from Bermuda and sold in Boston as early as 1636 were sweet potatoes. The Swedish botanist Peter Kalm, who travelled in America in 1748 to study native plants, wrote that they "have a sweet and very agreeable taste . . . and they almost melt in the mouth. It is not long since they have been planted here. They are dressed in the same manner as common potatoes, and eaten either along with them, or by themselves."[92]

Apples

The crab apple was the only native apple tree in America, and it was good only for making verjuice, or vinegar. But the English brought with them both scions and apple seeds and at once planted their orchards, the first one of record being planted about 1625 on Boston's Beacon Hill. Seventeen years later Edward Johnson wrote, "There are supposed to be in the Mattachusets (sic) Government at this day, neer a thousand acres of land planted for Orchards and Gardens. . . ."[93]

In those days when there was a sense of continuity and worth in the simple tasks of planting and harvesting, Joshua Hempsted entered into his Diary for Feb. 5, 1745/46, "I Toppled the Stockyard fence behind Trumans & Cut down one part of the Crotched old apple-tree near their pairtree, a very old Tree. I Concluded the Same age of the

Peartree both of my Grandfathers planting who lived but Seven year after the Town was first Settled wch was in 1646. 99 year ago in January."[94]

Trees grown from seeds produce fruit well enough, but frequently quite unlike the apple from which the seeds came. Farmers speak of the tree having returned to the wild, and the fruit is often smaller and more sour than that from the parent tree, but sometimes the result is quite the opposite and we hear of a farmer "discovering" a wonderful new apple. The Russett was such an apple "discovered" in Roxbury, Massachusetts, in the mid-1600's. The Pippin came from Long Island and was popular throughout the colonies. Ben Franklin had some Pippins sent to him in London in 1759, where they became quite the rage and resulted in giving America a good export product. The Rhode Island Greening grew first from seed in 1748 at Green's End near Newport and is still preferred by many cooks because it makes an excellent pie. The Baldwin came from a chance seedling in Wilmington, Massachusetts in 1740. This was an especially popular apple both for its taste and for its keeping qualities, an important consideration in early days.[95]

To store, apples might be buried in sand in the cellar or packed with straw in barrels, but the method shown in historic houses where some culinary activities are part of the program is the most evocative and fragrant. And that is, cut into slices, strung on strings and hung to dry. Apples that were less than perfect were made into apple sauce and apple butter. Even peels and cores were used in brewing a kind of beer which, when fermenting, formed a froth that could be used as yeast.

Apple Pie: "Apple dishes of one kind or another could be found at practically every colonial meal, especially in New England."[95] We read of apple slump, apple-mose, apple-crowdy, apple-tarts, mess apple-pies and puff apple-pies. Among all the apple dishes known to us and to the colonial household, apple pie has to be the best loved, and although every cook has her favorite recipe, we will make room for yet one more.

Apples: use Greenings, Jonathan, Duchess, or some other
tart variety.
3/4 to 1 cup sugar
2 Tbsp. flour

78

1/2 to 1 tsp. cinnamon
Dash of nutmeg, Dash of salt
6 to 7 apples, thinly sliced
2 Tbsp. butter
Pastry for 2-crust pie
Slice your apples. Mix dry ingredients and sprinkle over
apples, and mix throughout them; then place all into pastry
lined pie plate. Dot top with butter. Lay top crust over, cutting a design for steam to escape through. Seal edges with
tines of fork. Bake at 400 degrees F. for 45 to 50 minutes.

Mrs. Simmons would have *Apple Pie* made so:

Stew and strain the apples, to every three pints, grate the peel
of a fresh lemon, add cinnamon, mace, rosewater and sugar
to your taste—and bake in paste No. 3.

Her paste No. 3 is given here only as a curiosity, for there is more between the lines than on them and a good modern pie crust recipe
would be a much safer undertaking.

Paste No. 3: To any quantity of flour, rub in three fourths of
its weight in butter. For each peck of this misture use 12 eggs
and rub in one third or half of them, and roll in the rest.

On the *errata* page she tells us "for 12 eggs read 6." But since
she was writing for her contemporaries, not for us, she never
explains the difference between rubbing and rolling. We
must also be careful in altering the number of eggs since colonial chickens did not produce such large ones as modern,
chemically fed chickens are capable of.

Ignoring her crust recipe, we may still find her *Buttered Apple Pie*
worthy of imitation:

Pare, quarter, and core tart apples. Lay in paste . . . cover
with same; bake half an hour, when drawn (from oven) gently raise the top crust, add sugar, butter, cinnamon, mace,
wine or rose-water.

My mother made apple pie by that method minus the wine and rosewater, and, how she managed to get the top crust off and then on again without its breaking always roused much wonder when we had company. It was done very gingerly. By adding the sugar and spices after baking, Mother thought she achieved a better flavor, and she also liked the applesauce texture gained by stirring the apples after baking.

Apple Dumplings: Modern recipes for Apple Dumplings turn out what is essentially a baked apple encased in a baked pie crust, an excellent and hearty dessert or breakfast food, hot or cold. However, the old Apple Dumpling was truly a dumpling, cooked in a boiling pot.

Mrs. Simmons's Apple Dumpling
Put into paste, quartered apples, lye in a cloth and boil two hours, serve with sweet sauce.

Adapted Apple Dumpling
Prepare apples as for baked apples.
Prepare your favorite pie crust, roll and cut into squares large enough to enclose each apple individually. Set an apple into the center of a square of pastry. Fill the core hole with sugar and some cinnamon to flavor, top with a dab of butter. Bring corners of the square of pastry up to the top and seal. Place in individual, greased baking dishes, or all together in a greased baking dish, and bake at 400 degrees F. for 30 to 40 minutes. Serve with cold milk, or cream, or plain.

Apple Butter: It is a nippy but sunshiny October day and we must move away from the kitchen hearth with our colonial housewife while she makes her apple butter in the iron kettle hanging on the tripod over the outdoor fire. This is an all-day job with constant stirring absolutely essential, for otherwise the apple butter would stick to the bottom of the kettle, and burned apple butter is awful. One writer suggested that straw was sometimes put in the bottom of the kettle to prevent burning, but it is hard to imagine how this would work. Another seemingly more feasible method says that straw and water were placed in a larger kettle, with the smaller kettle of apples set into it to form a double boiler. Maybe caution was the best method, keeping the fire hot but not blazing, and being diligent with the stirring.

From the Journal of a young English woman residing in Middletown, Connecticut between 1796 and 1801 we read:

We had last week a very pleasant walk to a Cottage 3 miles and 1/2 from here. The good old Dame who owned it was very glad to see us but wondered much we cou'd walk so far —as soon as she saw us she said "why you hav'nt walked *clean* all the way from Middletown"! She treated us with some very good apples & cyder & some apple butter she had just been making and of which she said she had made 3 pails full . . . it was made something like apple sauce only boiled a very long time and no sugar to it.[96]

Modern Apple Butter
Boil down 2 gallons of cider to 1 gallon. Add 8 quarts of apples, pared and cut in quarters. Cook over low fire 4 to 5 hours. Add 6 cups sugar, 2 Tbsp. cinnamon, 1 tsp. each cloves & allspice. Stir constantly until thoroughly mixed through. Pack in hot, sterile jars, and seal. Makes about 12 pints.

For a super-easy method, here is the recipe from the Wells-Shipman-Ward House Tasting Day:

1 pint cider
6 lbs. apples.
   Cook the quartered, unpeeled apples in cider for 1/2 hour and put through food mill.
To resulting sauce add:
1-1/2 cups sugar
2 tsp. each cinnamon and allspice
1/8 tsp. cloves and 1/4 tsp. salt
   Mix well and place in shallow casserole and bake at 300 for 2 to 3 hours, stirring every half hour. Pack in clean jars when butter consistency is reached, and cover with melted paraffin. Makes 5 half-pint jars.

Treenware at the Stanley-Whitman House.

Berries and Quince

New England's fields and hills provided a summer procession of berries for boys and girls to pick and bring home to mother for preserves, conserves, jams, jellies, marmalades, syrups, wines, or for eating fresh. Nothing is sweeter than wild strawberries gathered into your aproned lap as you sit in a field mottled with berry plants and daisies and buttercups. Nothing is sweeter than picking your way among the thorny bushes under a cottony cloud sky in hot July to gather raspberries and currants. There's the best clump just out of reach, and there's a flash of orange as Scarlet Tanager flits away relinquishing his banquet to us. Summer moves on and we pick through blackberry brambles to elderberry shrub, and we move up the hillside with the season for huckleberries and blueberries. And nothing is sweeter than the ripe berry that steals its way into your mouth instead of the pail, except perhaps the pails you carry home filled with a crop from God's own garden. The industrious of God's elect gathered and gladly gave thanks for New England's abundance.

Today there are property rights to deprive us of the joy of gathering wild berries, but still we may savor the joys of laying up summer's richness in jeweled jars to sparkle in winter's drear. As previously reported, Abigail Foote recorded in her Journal: "I did housework in the forenoon and I wove in the afternoon and went with Ellen a-strawberrying."[97] She did not add how she prepared her berries that evening. Maybe she served a dish of them with milk or cream, or maybe a cobbler or shortcake with biscuit baked in the Dutch oven. Flummery was a popular dish made with blueberries, raspberries or strawberries.

Blueberry Flummery: Wash 4 cups of blueberries, put them into a saucepan with 1 cup of sugar, cook over low heat to simmering point, and continue cooking for ten minutes.

Butter 8 slices of bread generously, trimming crusts. Line a baking dish with the bread, pour a portion of the berries and juice over the bread and continue to alternate layers of bread and fruit, ending with fruit.

Bake at 350 degrees F. for 20 minutes. Chill well. Serve with whipped cream flavored with nutmeg.

Blueberry Slump: called on Cape Cod *Grunt*.

Cook 2 cups of blueberries with 1/2 cup of sugar and 1 cup of water. When boiling, drop spoonsful of dumpling batter into the sauce, and cook 10 minutes uncovered, 10 minutes covered. Serve with cream, whipped or not.

Josselyn called blueberries Bill Berries, noting there were two kinds, Black and Sky Coloured. He wrote of them:

"They usually eat of them put into a Bason, with Milk, and sweetned a little more with Sugar and Spice, or for cold Stomachs, in Sack. The Indians dry them in the Sun, and sell them to the English by the Bushell, who make use of them instead of Currence, putting of them into Puddens, both boyled and baked, and into Water Gruel."[98]

Blackberry Jelly: Alma DeForest Curtiss kept a recipe book dated 1839.[99] Among a few bread and cake recipes are many jelly and preserve recipes, which was often the case with a housewife's book of receipts. She easily remembered her everyday dishes, but the once-a-year speciality she was likely to forget, especially when proportions were important, as with jellies. Mrs. Curtiss made Currant Jelly, Peach and Quince Preserves, Apple Jelly, Quince Marmalade, Blackberry, Grape, Quince, and Crab Apple Jelly, Strawberry Sweetmeats, Preserved Citron, Currant Wine, Raspberry Vinegar, and Blackberry Cordial. Since we now have pectins to guarantee that our jams and jellies jell, we need not adapt these old recipes, but, as a sample, here is Mrs. Curtiss's *Blackberry Jelly:*

To 1 quart of juice, add 1 pound loaf sugar. Boil till hard.

Grape ketsup: Amelia Simmons used her fruits and berries in tarts more than in pies. She stewed and sugared her fruits, put them into a paste, and baked gently. She made tarts of cranberries, apricots, orange and lemon, gooseberry, and grape. Except for apple and currant pies, Amelia's pies are of meat. She also gives many rules for preserves, marmalades, and pickles, for "skill in preserving was ever an English-woman's pride, and New English did not forget the lessons learned in their 'faire English homes.'"

Pick over 5 pounds of grapes. Put into a saucepan with only the water that clings to them. Cook until the skins burst. Add: 2-1/2 pounds sugar, 1/2 tsp. salt, 1 Tbsp. each pepper, ground cinnamon, cloves, and allspice. Boil down to desired consistency. Put into sterilized jars and store in a cool place. Use with fish and shellfish. Makes 6 or 7 pints.

Cranberry Sauce: Josselyn said the cranberry was also called the Bearberry "because the bears use much to feed upon them" adding that "The Indians and English use them much boyling them with Sugar for Sauce to eat with their meat; and it is a delicate Sauce, especially for roasted Mutton; Some make tarts with them as with Goose Berries."[113]

The "delicate sauce" comes to us so conveniently today, already made, conforming to the manufactured shape of the can, that we deny ourselves the tangy aroma, the sound of the popping berries and the honest taste of homemade *Cranberry Sauce*:

> In a saucepan bring 2 cups of water and 2 cups of sugar to a boil. Add 4 cups of whole cranberries, and boil till they pop. Chill and serve with roast turkey.

In her cookbook *The American Frugal Housewife*, 1833, Lydia Maria Child advised that adding a pint of cranberries to a quart of batter pudding and boiling 3/4 of an hour made it a little stiffer than usual. It is, she wrote, "very nice, eaten with a sweet sauce."

> A modern *Cranberry Pudding*
> Combine 1/2 cup bread crumbs, 1/2 cup brown sugar, 2/3 cup finely chopped suet, and 1 cup cranberries with 1/3 cup milk. Sift together 1 cup sifted flour, 2 tsp. baking powder, 1/2 tsp. salt, and add the first mixture to the flour mixture. Mix. Pour into greased mold 2/3 full, cover tightly, place on rack with 1" of boiling water, and steam for 2 hours, high boil to start, then lower when steam begins to escape. Serve with a sweet sauce.

Preserved Quince: An old-time fruit which is seldom seen nowadays is the quince. Its hard yellow fruit, so velvety to the touch, so nippy to the smell, ripens last of all the fruits in the fall. It is good as sauce and as jelly, and old recipes often recommend adding a few quinces to your applesauce. Mrs. Simmons's rule for preserving quinces:

> Take a peck of Quinces, put them into a kettle of cold water, hand them over the fire, boil them till they are soft, then take them out with a fork, when cold pare them, quarter or halve them if you like; take their weight of loaf sugar, put into a bell-metal kettle or sauce pan, with one quart of water, scald and skim it till it is very clean, then put in your Quinces, let them boil in the sirrup for half an hour, add oranges (two, cut up) if you like, then put them in stone pots for use.

Chestnuts

October brings the race between children and squirrels for the year's last crop, the nuts. Crisp, cool days arrive, and boys have an excuse to throw nuts or stones at robber squirrel. Knock down the tenacious nut. Climb the tree and shake the branch. Oh, delicious freedom and delicious morsel cracked open to remember in winter the deliciously bright gathering days!

Hannah Glasse, author of *The Art of Cookery Made Plain and Easy*, 1796, gave the following recipe *To roast a Fowl with Chestnuts.*

First take some chesnuts, roast them very carefully, so as not to burn them; take off the skin and peel them; take about a dozen of them cut small, and bruise them in a mortar; parboil the liver of the fowl, bruise it, cut about a quarter of a pound of ham or bacon, and pound it; then mix them all together, with a good deal of parsley chopped small, a little sweet herbs, some mace, pepper, salt, and nutmeg; mix these together and put into your fowl, and roast it. The best way of doing it is to tie the neck, and hang it up by the legs to roast with a string, and baste it with butter. For sauce, take the rest of the chesnuts peeled and skinned; put them into some good gravy, with a little white wine, and thicken it with a piece of butter rolled in flour; then take up your fowl, lay it in the dish, and pour in the sauce. Garnish with lemon.

Salads

Fresh and cooked vegetables were used in salad, or *sallets*, throughout the colonial period. Gervase Markham gave recipes for both simple and compound sallats in his *English Huswife*, originally published in 1615. A simple salad was made of "washed greens, scallions, radish-roots, all young lettice, Cabage lettice, and boiled carrots, turneps, onions, beans, sparagus, and cucumbers, with such like served up simply without any thing but a little Vinegar, Sallet-Oyle, and Sugar.''

Compound Sallets were made of ''all manner of wholesome hearbes at their first springing, as Red Sage, Mints, Lettice, Violets, Marigolds, Spinage, and many others mixed together, then served up to the Table with Vinegar, Sallet Oyle and Sugar.'' And to ''serve at great feasts, and upon Princes tables,'' though there were indeed few of these in New England, he would add ''blancht Almonds, raisins, figs, and Capers.''[102]

From an English cookbook of 1650 we learn to make a ''sallet of Rose-Buds and Clove Gillyflowers. Pick Rose-Buds and put them in an earthen pipkin, with White Wine Vinegar and Sugar; so may you use Cowslips, Violets or Rosemary-flowers.''[103]

A word of caution for anyone using flowers: consult an herbal to be sure of the identities and qualities of your plant. The old ''marigold'' is the flower we designate ''calendula'' (*calendula officinals*) and is delightful in a green salad. The common marigold of our gardens is the African marigold and is poisonous, as is the common buttercup.

Chowders

I can think of nothing that hits the spot better on a cold day than a bowl of chowder for lunch or supper. Big chunks of clam and little cubes of potato, transparent bits of onion, a big glob of butter melting in the middle—mmm, bliss! And on Thanksgiving Day noon, when everybody is pestering the cook and dinner is still a traditional three or four hours away, the best of all possible stays of hunger is a bowl of corn chowder. I'll even opt for a bowl of chowder on a hot summer day when lettuce leaves and cold lemonade have failed to satisfy, provided it's been made already and is just waiting to be reheated. The aging, by the way, is the secret of a good chowder. Down in Maine, where you'll find experts on the subject, no self-respecting cook would ever serve a lobster stew less than 48 hours after she'd made it, and chowder likewise, though 24 hours will do to mingle the flavors.

Milch cows came to America on the *Charity* in 1624. By 1627, there were seven cows and twice as many goats in the settlement.[104] They were held in common and their milk shared, even after the allotment of 1627 when they were given to specified groupings of families. Milk was not in great supply those first years, but in time there was plenty, and bless the woman who, instead of using stock in her soup used milk and gave us this heavenly concoction.

It is, of course, possible that New England chowder is descended from *la chaudiere* of France, celebrating the safe return of the fishing fleet, when each man threw his fishy offering into the great pot to cook into a communal feast. The tradition came to the new world with the French fishermen of Acadia and eventually to New England, some say.

Any New Englander will tell you quahogs make the best chowder (even Rhode Islanders agree on that), and no New Englander will let a tomato anywhere near a clam chowder.

New England Clam Chowder
    1 pint quahogs chopped
    1 pint quahog liquor strained
    3 potatoes, peeled & diced
    1 onion, chopped
    1/4 lb. salt pork, diced
    1-1/2 quarts milk (some cream may be used)
    Salt & pepper to taste.
    Your choice of herbs, thyme recommended.
    Sauté salt pork until crisp, drain & set aside. Simmer onion in same pan until limp. Put diced potatoes in pot with onions and water to cover. Simmer until tender. Add quahogs, liquor, salt pork and seasonings. Finally add milk, which has been heated to somewhere near the same temperature. Stir while adding. Never boil a chowder.

New England Corn Chowder
    1/3 cup diced salt pork
    1 medium onion
    3 cups peeled, diced potatoes

2-1/2 c. cream style canned corn (No. 2 can)
1 tsp. salt, 1/8 tsp. pepper
2 cups rich milk
Cook salt pork in chowder kettle till crisp. Remove from pan. Add onion to fat and saute till slightly browned. Add boiling water and potatoes. Cover and cook till potatoes are tender. Add corn, milk, and seasonings. Simmer gently till well blended. (Use only enough water to come to top of potatoes —do not pour it off unless you think too much is left when you are ready to add corn and milk.)

Lobster Stew, The Perfect Nectar
Josselyn reported that lobsters grew to 20 pounds. A modern 1-1/4 pounder will make a stew for four people. Boil your lobster and remove the meat immediately, saving also the tomalley, the coral, and the thick white substance from inside the shell. Simmer the tomalley and coral in 1/2 cup butter for 7 or 8 minutes. Use a heavy chowder kettle. Then add the lobster meat, cut into fairly large pieces. Cook all together 10 min. over low heat. Remove from heat and *cool slightly*. Then add, *very slowly*, a trickle at a time, 1 quart rich milk, stirring constantly. *Allow to age* from 6 to 48 hours before reheating to serve. (Italicized directions are the secrets to the perfect Lobster Stew.) Serve with chowder crackers and dill pickles.

Seafood

Baked Shad: When the shadbush fluffs up the muddy landscape and adder's tongue nods yellow along rushing brooks, we know in New England that spring has come. At this time some primordial voice calls to the shad and salmon to make their spawning run up tidal rivers.

And this is the time to take them. My father always made a trip to Enfield Dam for his roe-shad and gave the roe to his maiden sister, while we had to be content with the bony meat baked. Mother stuffed it with bread stuffing, laid salt pork over it, covered it tight, baked it long and slow (250 degrees F. for about 5 or 6 hours), and the bones all "melted" to become edible.

Cooked Eel: From the Connecticut River Dad also brought home an eel which he had to cook for himself because Mother was squeemish and claimed its cut-up sections still quivered in milk in the big iron skillet. Everyone knew Mother's opinion of anything on the order of snake, and Grandma had a special, one-quart blue graniteware pail with a lid and bail in which she often brought one serving of eel when she came to call.

My father and his mother cut his cleaned eel in 2" to 3" pieces, washed and wiped them dry, rolled them in flour, browned them lightly in salt pork fat in the iron skillet and then added milk and heated all through.

Our ancestors made more of a production out of it. Josselyn reported that the common way to cook eels was "to boil them in half water half wine with the bottom of a manchet (loaf of wheat bread), a fagot of parsley and a little Winter Savory, when they are boiled they take them out and break the bread in the broth and put in two or three spoonfuls of yest and a piece of sweet butter, pour to the eals laid upon sippets (toast)."

However, Josselyn added, "I fancie my way better which is this: After the Eals are flay'd and washed I fill their bellies with nutmeg grated and cloves a little bruised and sow them up with a needle and thread; then I stick a clove here and there in their sides about an inch asunder, making holes for them with a bodkin (similar to a hat pin); this done I wind them up in a wreath and put them in a kettle with half water and half wine vinegar, so much as will rise four fingers above the Eals; in midst of the Eals I put the bottom of a penny white loaf and a fagot of these herbs following, Parsley, one handful, a little sweet Marjoram, Penniroyal, and Savory, a branch of Rosemary, bind them up with a thread and when they are boiled enough take out the Eals and pull out the thred that their bellies were sewed up with, turn out the Nutmeg and Cloves; put the Eals in a dish with butter and vinegar upon a chafing dish with coals to keep warm, then put into the broth three or four spoonfuls of good ale-yeast with the juice of half a lemon; but before you put in your Yeast beat it in a porringer with some of the broth, then break the crust of bread very small and mingle it well together with the broth, pour it into a deep dish and garnish it with the other half of the Lemon, and so serve them up to the Table in two dishes.''[105]

Sieve or flour-sifter, made with the tail hair of
a horse and woven into a wooden frame.

Maine Salmon and Peas: Salmon were so plentiful in New England streams that a clause was sometimes written into an apprentice's agreement prohibiting the master from serving salmon to the boy more often than two times a week. After the Revolution, salmon, new peas, and new potatoes became the proper meal with which to celebrate the Fourth of July, and farmers planted early and watched with expectancy to be sure to have ''peas for the Fourth.'' Hot dogs seem to have shoved the salmon aside except down in Maine, where it is still part of the tradition.

Maine Salmon and Peas

Wrap a piece of Salmon (3 or 4 pounds, head end is best) in cheesecloth. Lower it into a kettle and pour two quarts court boullion, heated, over the fish. Simmer, do not boil, over low heat for 25 minutes. While it is cooking, boil the peas (3 cups shelled) and the potatoes (12 to 16 small new potatoes with or without jackets) separately in enough salted water to cover. Lift fish from kettle, remove the skin and place fish in center of a large hot platter. Arrange the potatoes and peas around it, pour egg sauce over the salmon, butter the vegetables, garnish with parsley.

Egg Sauce

Make a cream sauce of 4 Tbsp. butter, 4 Tbsp. flour, 2 cups of milk. Season with salt and pepper, and juice of half a lemon. Add 2 hardcooked eggs, diced fine.

Court Boullion

3 Tbsp. butter	2 springs parsley, minced
1 onion, minced	1 quart boiling water
1 stalk celery, minced	1 bay leaf
1 carrot, chopped	8 whole cloves
1/2 cup vinegar	4 peppercorns

Melt butter in a skillet, add vegetables and sauté for 5 minutes. Add remaining ingredients and boil for 5 minutes. Strain.

Oysters: Oysters were dearly loved in the early days. Madam Knight noted on October 7, 1704, when she arrived in New Haven, "There are great plenty of Oysters all along by the sea side, as farr as I Rode in the Collony, and those very good." And Joshua Hempsted spent an afternoon with his daughter and son-in-law Miner at Stonington, where they all went "to widow Miners at the Seaside to Eat oysters etc." One can imagine the happy time the young couple and both in-laws had that May day in 1740. (Oysters are more hardy and have a better flavor in the cooler months, from September through April. It has long been a dictum that one eats oysters only during those months whose spelling includes an *r*. This was simply an easy way to remember and was never legislated. Oystermen and fish mongers found they did not keep well in non-*r* months; thus it was economically unsound to bring them to market. As a child I had a secret wonderment about the ability of the oyster to spell, but, though the oyster knows nothing about when he tastes best, he does know that he spawns during warm weather, so for the sake of conservation there is a further reason for not taking them from May through August.)

Old cookbooks present a variety of ways to serve oysters: fried oysters, oyster pancakes, oyster pie, scalloped oysters. Mrs. Simmons would have you smother a fowl in oysters:

Fill the bird with dry Oysters, and sew up and boil in water just sufficient to cover the bird, salt and season to your taste — when done tender, put into a deep dish and pour over it a pint of stewed oysters, well buttered and peppered, garnish a turkey with springs of parsley or leaves of celery: a fowl is best with a parsley sauce.

Scalloped Oysters (modern)
1/2 cup bread crumbs   1 cup cracker crumbs
1/4 cup melted butter   salt and pepper
1 pint shucked oysters   oyster liquor
2 cups milk or   (at least 4 Tbsp.)
   light cream

Mix bread and cracker crumbs and stir in melted butter. Put a thin layer of crumbs in bottom of a buttered, shallow baking dish. Cover with oysters, sprinkle with salt and pepper. Add half the oyster liquor and half the milk. Repeat, and cover top with remaining crumbs. Bake in a hot oven (400 degrees F) about 30 minutes. Serves 4.

Oyster Stew
1 quart fine oysters with liquor
1 pint rich milk (add some cream if not rich)
pepper and salt to taste
real butter
Heat liquor to boiling and add oysters and simmer softly for 5 minutes or until edges of oysters curl. Add milk and heat just

to boiling point, no more. Add seasoning, take up into shallow soup bowls and top with large piece of butter. Serve with oyster crackers. Serves 4.

Cod: The seafood that spells New England to most Americans nowadays is probably lobster, but for generations New Englanders preferred cod. The cod fisheries were so important to the economy of the region that in 1784 Massachusetts called it "sacred" and hung a five foot sculpture of a cod in the State House on Beacon Hill. It is still there. Codfish was the traditional Saturday night supper into modern times, and one twentieth century Connecticut bride who had been fed codfish every Saturday of her single life set her husband's fresh trout to soak overnight "to draw the salt out."

Cape Cod Turkey
1 pound salt codfish
1/4 pound salt pork
8 medium potatoes
Freshen cod by covering with cold water, bring to boiling point but do not allow to boil. Pour off water. Repeat at least three times, taste to tell when it is no longer too salty. In last water cook over low heat for 10 minutes. While cod is freshening, dice salt pork and render over low heat until light brown. Peel and boil the potatoes. Put the hot, boiled potatoes into a deep serving dish and place pieces of codfish over them. Pour a cup of medium cream sauce over, top with crisp salt pork. Serves 4. Harvard beets are a traditional accompaniment.

Codfish Gravy or Creamed Codfish (for non-Cape Codders)
1/2 pound salt codfish
1 egg, beaten
Cream sauce made of 2 Tbsp. butter, 2 Tbsp. flour, 2 cup milk and 1/4 tsp. pepper.
Cut codfish into pieces, soak in water overnight to draw out the salt. Drain in the morning and simmer in fresh water for 10 minutes. Make cream sauce, pour a small amount of it into the beaten egg, stirring constantly, then mix the fish, egg, and sauce together and serve on hot buttered toast or hot boiled potatoes.

Codfish Cakes or Codfish Balls
2 cups salt codfish
2 cups mashed potatoes
1 egg white, beaten
cream

Soak codfish overnight. Pick apart into fine pieces. Cut potatoes into small pieces and boil together with the codfish.
When potatoes are done, mash them together and add the
beaten egg and enough cream to make mixture light and fluf-
fy. For balls drop by spoonsful into deep hot fat and fry till
light brown. For cakes pat into cakes and fry on a hot, lightly
greased griddle. Good with egg and curry cream sauce, or with
ketsup or horseradish.

Cape Cod Boiled Dinner: The Curator-Emeritus of the Plymouth Antiquarian Society sat in the barn-office at Harlow House in Plymouth
chatting about her experiences with open-hearth cooking. "You know
that lovely Cape Cod Boiled Dinner?" she asked, "the one where they
put the codfish in the center of the plate and then they pass the potatoes and beets and onions and carrots and they put them all around
the codfish, and it looks so pretty, then they take their fork and *muss*
it all up together and eat it, and it tastes so good? Well, I have a theory
on that dinner," she said. "I can't prove it but I think some Cape Cod
sea captain sailing to the other side of the world had a meal in India or
someplace where they have the curried chicken or lamb and all those
other things that go around it, the cocoanut and peanuts and fruits
and so on, and then they muss that up altogether. And I think he came
home and told his wife about it and she took it over and so started the
Cod Fish Dinner."

These things have to start somewhere. Certainly the lady has had
experience enough to draw a logical conclusion, and I like to believe
her. The Boiled Dinner is a long tradition on the Cape, where it is ap-
proached almost reverently.

Inland, the Boiled Dinner consists of a brisket of corned beef,
boiled potatoes, beets, carrots and cabbage, accompanied by horseradish and mustard and transformed the next day into Red Flannel
Hash.

Meat

"The proportion of animal food, eaten in this country, is, I think, excessive," observed Timothy Dwight during his travels in New England in the early nineteenth century. Is it any wonder? Besides their domestic pork, mutton and, by 1800, beef, colonists had all the game animals and birds of the nearby woodlands, so the fowling pieces seen hanging over the fireplaces at most of our historic houses could almost be called part of the equipment for preparing the meal.

Meats were roasted, stewed, minced, put into pies, and the methods of preparation were extremely lengthy and involved.

A book which was contemporary with the first colonists to New England and which they probably knew is *Country Contentments or the English Huswife* by Gervase Markham, first published in London in 1615. In the 1623 edition, Markham tells how *to make a good Pottage:*

> It resteth now that we speak of boild meats and broths, which forasmuch as our Hous-wife is intended to be generall, one that can as well feed the poore as the rich, we will first begin with those ordinarie wholsome boyld meates, which are of use in every good mans house; therefore to make the best ordinarie Pottage, you shall take a racke of Mutton cut into pieces, or a leg of Mutton cut into pieces; for this meate and these joynts are the best, although any other joynt, or any fresh Beefe will likewise make good Pottage: and having washt your meate well, put it into a cleane pot with faire water, and set it on the fire, then take Violet leaves, Succory, Strawbery leaves, Spinage, Langdebeefe, Marigold flowers, Scallions, & a little Parsly, & chop them very small together; then take half so much Oat-meale well beaten as there is Hearbs, and mixe it with the Hearbs, and chop all very well together: then when the pot is ready to boyle, skum it very wel, and then put in your hearbs, and so let it boyle with a quick fire, stirring the meate oft in the pot, till the meate bee boyld enough, and that the hearbs and water are mixt to-

gether without any separation, which will bee after the consumption of more than a third part: Then season them with Salt, and serve them up with the meate either with Sippets or without.[106]

Carbonados: We are shown racks for the broiling of meat at some of the historic houses, and of course we think of our own broiled steaks and chops, but that is not what seventeenth century broiled meat was like. The animals were tougher than ours, the meat-cutting was different, and the preparation, according to Markham, was as follows:

Of Carbonados, which is meate broiled upon the Coales (and the invention thereof first brought out of France, as appeares by the name) are of divers kinds according to mens pleasures: for there is no meate either boiled or roasted whatsoever, but may afterwards bee broiled, if the Master thereof be disposed; yet the generall dishes for the most part which are used to be Carbonadoed, are a Breast of Mutton halfe boyled, a Shoulder of Mutton halfe roasted, the Leggs, Wings, and Carkases of Capon, Turkie, Goose, or any other Fowle whatsoever, especially Land-Fowle. And lastly, the uppermost thick skinne which covereth the ribbes of Beefe, and is called (being broiled) the skin of Court Goose, and is indeed a dish used most for wantonnesse, sometimes to please appetite: to which may also be added the broyling of Pigs heads, or the graines of any Fowle whatsoever after it is roasted and drest.[107]

Pigeons: In her 1807 book, *New System of Domestic Cookery*, Mrs. Maria Eliza Rundell tells *How to Fricasee Pigeons:*

Quarter each pigeon and fry them. Take also some green pease, and fry them also till they be like to burst. Then pour boiling water upon them, and season the liquor with pepper, salt, onions, garlic, parsley and vinegar. Thicken with yolks of eggs.

Pork, Ham: Nothing was wasted from any animal. Consider, for example, the results of butchering one hog. There are the hams, loins and shoulders, all good for smoking and roasting. There is bacon. However, Timothy Dwight wrote in 1821 that only the hams, shoulders and cheeks of pork were "converted into bacon (i.e. were smoked). I do not know," he adds, "that I ever saw a flich of bacon, cured in New-England, in my life. The sides of the hog (the bacon) are here always pickled; and by the New England people are esteemed much superior to bacon."[108] The feet were pickled. The head, with the tail thrown in for good measure, was cooked up for headcheese. The fat became salt pork, without which a New England woman could scarcely keep house. All scraps went toward making sausage, which was then packed into the cleaned intestines used for casings.

Sausage: Mrs. Curtiss of Watertown, Connecticut started with 50 pounds of pork when making sausage, and added:

> 1 pound and a quarter of salt
> 10 ounces loaf sugar
> 4 ounces pepper
> 1 ounce salt petre
> 8 ounces sage.

Besides adding flavor to beans, corn chowder and many, many other dishes, salt pork made a meal in itself, as

Salt Pork Gravy
Fry up about 3/4 of a pound of salt pork, cut in cubes. Remove them from pan. Leave about 2 Tbsp. fat in the pan, add 2 Tbsp. flour and blend. Add 1 cup cold milk. Heat. Add pork slices (or cubes) and serve over hot baked or boiled potatoes.

Mince Pie: Lydia Maria Child, who wrote "Over the river and through the Woods," also wrote a cookbook from which we take the recipe for *Mince Pies.*

Boil a tender, nice piece of beef—any piece that is clear from sinews and gristle; boil it till it is perfectly tender. When it is cold, chop it very fine, and be very careful to get out every particle of bone and gristle. The suet is sweeter and better to boil half an hour or more in the liquor the beef has been boiled in; but few people do this. Pare, core, and chop the apples fine. If you use raisins, stone them. If you use currants, wash and dry them at the fire. Two pounds of beef, after it is chopped; three quarters of a pound of suet; one pound and a quarter of sugar; three pounds of apples; two pounds of currants, or raisins. Put in a gill of brandy; lemon-brandy is better, if you have any prepared. Make it quite moist with new cider. I should not think a quart would be too much; the more moist the better, if it does not spill out into the oven. A very little pepper . . . One ounce of cinnamon, one ounce of cloves. Two nutmegs add to the pleasantness of the flavor; and a bit of sweet butter put upon the top of each pie, makes them rich; but these are not necessary. Baked three quarters of an hour. If your apples are rather sweet, grate in a whole lemon.[109]

Baby tender, Whipple House.

This recipe makes a great plenty of mincemeat, which could be kept in a crock covered with a layer of rendered beef suet or lard which would harden like paraffin in the cool buttery. Mrs. Child may also have intended that a large number of pies be made at one time, which was a New England custom.

Mrs. Simmons directed this in her Minced Pie recipe. "Weeks after, when you have occasion to use them, carefully raise the top crust, and with a round edg'd spoon, collect the meat into a basin, which warm with additional wine and spices to the taste of your circle, while the crust is also warm'd like a hoe cake, put carefully together and serve up, by this means you can have hot pies through the winter, and enrich'd singly to your company."[110]

Cakes

Hartford Election Cake: Connecticut's most famous cake is Election Cake, made once a year to be served, some say, to those who voted a straight ticket, or according to others, to any guests who came by on Election Day. Madam Knight in 1704 reported of the people of Connecticut, "Their Chief Red Letterday is St. Election, which is annually observed according to Charter, to choose their Goven[r]." About a hundred years later another traveller through Connecticut, Edward Augustus Kendall, published the account of his trip, reporting at length on the election procession, the election sermon, the swearing-in and the two election balls.

> The election-day is a holiday throughout the state and even the whole remainder of the week is regarded in a similar light. Servants and others are now in some measure indemnified for the loss of the festivals of Christmas, Easter, and Whitsuntide which the principles of their church deny them. Families exchange visits, and treat their guests with slices of election-cake; and thus preserve some portion of the luxuries of the forgotten feast of the Epiphany.[111]

Hartford Election Cake is served at Noah Webster's Birthday Party celebrated every fall at the lexicographer's birthplace in West Hartford. From numerous recipes I have chosen the one used for the 1976 baking contest was sponsored by the Association of Connecticut Fairs. It corresponds quite closely to other variations, though the Noah Webster recipe calls for the addition of 1/2 cup of brandy.

Hartford Election Cake

2 cups milk, heated	2 eggs
3/4 cup soft butter	5 to 5-1/2 cups flour
1/2 cup brown sugar	1-1/2 cups raisins
1-1/2 cups white sugar	1/2 cup citron
3/4 tsp. salt	1/2 tsp. nutmeg
2 pkgs. active dry yeast	1/2 tsp. mace

Place warm milk, sugar and salt in mixing bowl. Add yeast, 4 cups flour, butter, and eggs. Beat at medium speed 2 minutes. Add balance of ingredients and mix thoroughly. Batter should be slightly stiff. Pour into 2 greased bread pans (9'' x 5'' x 3'' deep). Allow to rise until double in bulk (approximately 2 hours). Bake at 350 degrees F for 50 minutes. Remove from pans immediately and cool on wire racks.[112]

Gingerbread: One of the delights issuing from the colonial oven was Gingerbread. Indeed, it had delighted medieval and Elizabethan appetites and does ours, too. It is good hot with cold applesauce on it or cider with it, or cold with whipped cream and a cup of hot tea on a winter's day, and on a summer's day with lemonade or cold milk. Anyway at all, it's better than Ambrosia to a Yankee.

In America, Gingerbread came to be associated with Muster, or Training Day, a day for the local militia to turn out on the village green and "exercise their arms." Required generally once a month, it became a holiday with the militia providing the spectacle and women the refreshment. The day began with roll-call and inspection, then came drilling, marching to fife and drum, loading, firing and hitting the mark. After review by local magistrates, came dismissal and merriment, and the village green became the scene of a picnic for all participants and spectators with gingerbread and cyder or gingerbread and rum.

Mrs. Holcomb of Watertown, Connecticut kept training day and gingerbread vividly in memory, and in her old age she wrote of her childhood around 1800 when the children ate "a hasty breakfast, and, dressed in their Sunday suits, and their pockets lined with coppers, were ready to proceed to the scene of action. Those coppers were designed to purchase gingerbread of a venerable old lady who lived near the liberty pole and always kept in readiness for such occasions. Oh, the flavor of that gingerbread on youthful lips! Methinks I taste it yet, and see the shining luster of its glossy surface."[113]

That last line tells us that this gingerbread was the thin, flat kind we associate with gingerbread men, the kind Benjamin Franklin bought on his way to Philadelphia, the kind Shakespeare wrote of and Hogarth pictured.[114] Most of the gingerbread recipes from colonial days are for this hard, "Militia Day" Gingerbread, and our first American cookbook, Mrs. Simmons's, gives four varieties of it, but also includes one for "Soft Gingerbread to be baked in pans," which is the cake-like gingerbread we enjoy today. When Mrs. Child wrote in 1833, she gave a recipe for each kind, recommending the hard as "good to have in the family, it keeps so well." Neither kind keeps very well in my family, but will disappear almost overnight.

Hard Gingerbread

2-1/2 cups flour, sifted	1 tsp. soda
1 tsp. ginger	3 Tbsp. boiling water
1/2 tsp. salt	1 cup molasses
3 Tbsp. butter	

Sift flour, ginger, salt together; work in the butter. Dissolve soda in water, add to molasses and stir in dry ingredients. Knead well. Let stand in cold place until dough is thoroughly chilled. Roll out on floured board to 3/4 inch, adding just enough flour so dough will roll. Bake at 375 degrees F for 20 min. Makes 2 sheets, 7" x 11". After baking, while gingerbread is still hot, glaze it with 3 tsp. milk mixed with 3 tsp. molasses (brush it on). Cut into inch squares.

Soft, or cake-like, Gingerbread

1/2 cup sugar	1 tsp. ginger

1/2 cup butter
1 egg
1 cup molasses
2-1/2 cups sifted flour
1-1/2 tsp. soda

1 tsp. cinnamon
1/2 tsp. cloves
1/2 tsp. salt
1 cup hot water

Cream sugar and butter, add egg, molasses, flour sifted with dry ingredients. Beat well. Add hot water last. Beat well again. (It will be thin.) Pour into 8" x 8" greased and floured pan and bake 1 hour at 350 degrees F.

Pound Cake: The other popular colonial cake was Pound Cake. Until the development of saleratus, and then baking soda and powder, cakes could not be made truly light the way we like them. Mrs. Tallmadge of Litchfield, Connecticut wrote down her recipe for pound cake, calling it *Queen's Cake*.

Take one pound of flour, one pound of butter, one pound of eggs, work your butter and sugar to a cream, then beat your eggs and mix with it. Then put in your flour, a Gill of Brandy and a Gill of Rosewater.

A Modern Version of Pound Cake
1 cup soft butter
1-1/2 cups sifted flour
1/4 tsp. baking soda
1-1/2 cup sugar
1-1/2 Tbsp. fresh lemon juice

1-1/2 tsp. vanilla
5 large eggs separated
1/8 tsp. salt
1 tsp. cream of tartar

Sift flour, soda and 3/4 cup sugar into a bowl. Cream butter, add egg yolks one at a time, lemon juice, vanilla and 3/4 cup sugar. Add flour mixture until well blended. Beat egg whites with salt till stiff but not dry. Fold in cream of tartar. Add to first mixture with spatula. Spoon into pan. Jolt pan to remove bubbles. Bake at 325 degrees F 1 hour. Turn off oven. Let stay in oven 10 to 15 minutes more.

Sweets and Sweetening Agents

In the herb garden behind the Putnam Cottage in Greenwich are straw bee skeps to furnish the family's honey. Bees were brought from England and set loose here to be fruitful and multiply. They produced their crop of honey in one season. Without bee skeps, a good husbandman found the hive in a tree hollow but never took more than a fair share, always leaving enough to see the bees through the winter.

Maple sugar and syrup making occupied the men through February and March. As the lengthening days warmed, sap began its rise in the trees. Now the husbandman had to be ready with the taps, or spiles, he had whittled in cold January. Four or five hundred spiles was usual for a farm family. They were whittled of sumac wood, and metal rods heated in the fire were used to burn through the pithy center of the sumac to make the spout.

The snow was still deep when it was time to tap the trees. Out to the sugar bush with the supplies he went to drill holes in the trunk of the maple, insert the spile and catch the trickling sap. Before 1800, hollowed-out log troughs were used to collect sap. The spile with bucket hung from it came into use about 1800. Goodrich describes sugaring as "wholly a domestic operation, and one in which the children rejoiced"[115] as they gathered and then boiled down the sap at the outdoor fire in the sugar bush, with the great kettles hanging from the pole stretched between two forked saplings. The run of sap would continue as long as the nights remained cold, but a fine, warm spring night marks the sap run's end.

Sometime before the equipment was packed away with the newly made product, time would be found for a Sugar-on-Snow Party. First the thick boiling syrup was taken up in a ladle and dribbled over a clean place on the snow, where sudden cold turned it into a waxy and chewy confection, delicious to eat with a pickle, to cut the sweet, and more candy to cut the sour.

Henry Wansey was fascinated by maple sugar when he was travelling through Connecticut in May 1794, but he found the flavor disappointing. At the tavern where he dined he wrote, "We had excellent provisions . . . three sorts of sugar brought always to the table; the muscovado (from sugar cane), the fine lump sugar, and the maple; from the novelty of it, I preferred the last, though I could not find much difference in the taste of it."[116] Something must have ailed Mr. Wansey's taste buds. Most New Englanders would subscribe to John Burrough's description, "It has a wild delicacy of flavor that no other sweet can match. What you smell in freshly cut maple wood, or taste in the blossom of the tree, is in it. It is then, indeed, the distilled essence of the tree . . . It is worthy the table of the gods."[117]

I have seen no sap buckets or spiles in the historic houses, and properly they do belong in the man's domain. Yet the product being food and the carving of the spiles a fireside industry, one might expect to see them. They are well exhibited at the Sloane-Stanley Museum of Home and Farm Tools in South Kent, Connecticut.

Molasses was a favorite sweetener no matter what one's economic or political views on the subject might be. In 1733 Parliament passed the Molasses Act designed to help owners of sugar plantations in the British West Indies by taxing, at 6 pence a gallon, molasses brought to America from any other source, such as the French West Indies. There was a strong resistance in the colonies, and British agents practiced a "salutary neglect" in the collection of this tax. Smuggling of molasses and many other products became a respectable business among the American colonists.

When George Grenville became the new British financial minister in 1763, the official attitude hardened, Grenville having discovered that the revenue service was costing four times what it took in. New legislation resulted, including the Sugar Act of 1764, which reduced the duty on molasses to three pence a gallon but provided for enforcement. One consequence for the colonists would be a shortage of specie which they had been getting through trade with Spanish and French West Indies. And since England forbad the colonists to issue paper money, colonial merchants faced a dire problem. The Sugar Act gave a boost to the resistance movement that led to the Revolution.

The Shaw Mansion in New London was built in 1756 for Captain Nathaniel Shaw, who with his son Nathaniel was engaged in shipping, trading and smuggling. They had agents in the West Indies, so out from New London went horses, lumber and provisions, and back came molasses and sugar.

Hippocras bag, used for straining when making beverages and medicines,
Ironmaster's House.

Politics aside, molasses was a desired sweetener in the home. How good it was, and is, on Hasty Pudding! And Indian Pudding is impossible without it. Children liked a little in their milk, and they liked to lick the spoon. As years went on, molasses cookies and molasses taffy flavored the atmosphere of the salt box homes.

At the Bush-Holley House in Cos Cob can be seen a cone of white sugar which a family of means would have reserved, even in this affluent home, for the special occasions. This was another West Indian import and usually came wrapped in a purple paper much treasured in itself for the dye it would make. A sugar devil, or sugar scissors, was employed to cut a chunk of sugar off the cone to make smaller pieces for sweetening the company cup of tea. Some say the sugar was held in the mouth and the tea allowed to pass over it, but that was a New York Dutch custom, not New England. (Since the Bush family originally came from New York, they may well have enjoyed their sugar and tea so.)

The English loved their sweets and even in the very early years of settlement they managed to have their marmalades and preserves. Edward Johnson wrote in 1642 that there was "a great plenty of wine and sugar" and that they had "apples, pears, and quince tarts instead of their former Pumpkin Pies."[118]

Josselyn recommended some provisions that would classify as sweets to be brought on the crossing "in case you, or any of yours should be sick at sea: Conserves of Roses, Clove-Gilly-flowers . . . Prunes to stew, Raisons of the Sun, Currence, Sugar . . ."[119]

Sucket, a favorite sweet of Queen Elizabeth's, was served throughout the colonial period, but with its name changed to sweetmeats in the eighteenth century. *Sucket* referred to both dried, sugared fruits and fruits preserved in a heavy syrup.[120] At the Webb House is an interesting piece of silver which the director believes may have been designed for eating sucket. It looks like a spoon and fork combination similar to those designed for campers today, though of an elegance for the parlor, not the campground. By removing the spoon from the handle and removing the pick from the opposite end of the handle, you would have an implement for eating the fruits, with a pick to help in removing pits. Then substituting the round-bowled spoon for the fork, you could sip the remaining syrup.

In the elaborate dinner of the well-to-do with the two courses of innumerable dishes, dessert became the grand climax, served on the bare table after the two "removes." At evening tea parties the dessert table was set up separately with its array of sweets surrounding an elevated piece such as a figurine holding up a bowl with fruits, or tiered plates holding glasses of sparkling jellies and frothy sillabubs. Then all about the center eye-catcher were bowls and plates of fruits and sweets to delight both eye and palate. John Adams described such a dessert table as "everything which could delight the eye or alure the taste."[121]

Markham starts his directions for making jellies, "take calves feet and wash them and scald of the haire as cleane as you can get it."[122] At this point, we leave him. Most of us feel we are going back to basics when we reach for the orange package of unflavored gelatin, and I would not recommend Markham on jelly to even the purest of the purists. Simply know when you serve jellies that your dessert has a noble lineage and rejoice that you don't have to start with calves feet.

The *Plum Pudding*, on the other hand, is worth the effort. Associated with Christmas in Old England, it was transferred to Thanksgiving in Puritan New England, where Christmas was not celebrated, in an effort to purify religion of all excesses. Thanksgiving also substituted the American turkey for the Christmas goose.

This is a pudding steamed in a pudding bag, and although pudding pans are readily available today, here are directions for using a Pudding Bag:

Start with about a 12" square of cloth such as unbleached muslin. Dampen it in warm water, wring it out and flour one side well. This is the side where you will lay your pudding batter. After you place your batter, bring up the corners of the bag and tie them with strong cord, allowing room for expansion of the pudding, for it will expand whether you allow for it or not, with disastrous results. When you tie your cord or string, leave a loop through which you can stick a long wooden spoon handle for lifting the pudding out of the boiling water. Be sure the water is boiling well in a large kettle when you lower your pudding into it. Cover the kettle and continue boiling constantly for the three hours required for pudding. If you have to add water, be sure it is boiling before you add it. When the cooking time has elapsed, remove the pudding from the water to a large plate and at once remove the pudding from the bag. Serve the pudding hot, whether with a sauce or with brandy poured over and set aflame. For Christmas, place a sprig of holly on your pudding plate for show.

A (comparatively) modern Plum Pudding
1 cup suet, chopped or ground fine
1 cup molasses
1 cup milk
3 cups flour
1 cup raisins
1 tsp. salt
1 tsp. soda
1/2 tsp. cloves
1 tsp. each cinnamon and nutmeg
some citron or mixed fruit if desired
Mix all together, place in greased pudding pan (or bag) and steam about 3 hours.

Tea

Is it possible that the country that launched its independence with a midnight, harbor-wide tea party is the same whose fashionable residents, when first brewing tea, threw out the liquid only to butter, salt and eat the leaves? Incredible, yet the story is so told.

Tea, coffee and chocolate were all introduced to England in the early seventeenth century and to America soon afterwards. Coffee gained popularity first, because of the three it was least expensive. "Coffee houses" soon became popular gathering places to enjoy the beverage and conviviality. Tea was at first used medicinally for headaches and a number of other vague symptoms, but by the end of the century it had become a social drink, and while coffee remained with politics in the coffeehouses, tea was drunk at home at breakfast and in the afternoon with gatherings of family and friends. It was still expensive, as was the equipage with which to serve it, so it became a status symbol, and some families had group portraits painted of their tea parties.[123] By mid-century the cost had dropped, the middle class took up the custom and tea caught on among rural as well as urban people throughout the colonies.

Teapots and tea canisters were basic items along with cups and saucers, teaspoons, tongs, a sugar container, a milk container and the slop bowl. In the early 1700s, tea sets were ceramic. Towards the end of the century, silver sets were available, and just as today, some people bought individual pieces rather than matched sets.

The custom was for the tea tray to be brought to the hostess, who was seated near the fireplace where a kettle of hot water waited on a trivet. From the tea caddy, which was a wooden cabinet holding the canisters of tea, the hostess chose her tea: Hyson, Souchong, or Congo; Bohea, Pekoe, Green, or Imperial. Using the top of the canister for a measure, she put the proper amount of her desired blend into her pot. Then, taking the kettle from the maid, she poured the hot water over her tea. To pour the brewed tea into cups she now needed a strainer and probably used the same one she had been using with her punch bowl all those years before the new oriental drink became the fad. So filling her cups, she offered her guests sugar, taking with her tongs one of the pieces broken previously in the kitchen from the cone.

Those leaves left in the strainer had to be disposed of, so they went into the slop bowl, as did any dregs left in a cup when the second, third, fourth or fifth cupsful were presented. When a guest turned his handless cup upside down in the saucer and placed his spoon across the cup's bottom, Madam Hostess knew her guest had a sufficiency. For her to urge him to have more would be as bad manners as for him to refuse more before he had turned over his cup. The cup's position told all, and pity the pour soul of whom the story is told that after twelve cups he finally hid his empty cup in his pocket to prevent his hostess from refilling it yet one more time.

The cups were handleless and saucers were deep, which was the style throughout the eighteenth century. Cups having handles at that time were for coffee and chocolate. "Saucer-sipping, while it may have been common among the general public, was frowned upon by polite society."[124]

The teapots of the early eighteenth century were plump and pear-shaped and generally of ceramic. The inverted pear was the new shape for mid-century and is the type shown in the Copley portrait of Paul Revere (1768–70), from which we may judge that silver was then the desired material. At the end of the century the straight-sided, oval pot was the fashion.

A round tea table in the parlor at the Silas Deane House in Wethersfield is set for tea. The brass kettle is on a trivet at the fireplace. The party is in progress, for one guest has indicated his satisfaction by placing his cup upside-down in the saucer, his silver spoon across the bottom. Other cups await filling. Mistress Dean's two chinaware tea canisters stand near her teapot, slop bowl and sugar bowl. Out in the kitchen are the sugar scissors and the cone of sugar from which more can be cut.

Along with the "dish of tea" there might be served cakes, cold pastries, sweetmeats, preserved fruits, or even plates of cracked nuts. The guests could stand or sit. Some might go, others would come, and the tea party went on and on.

In 1773, the fad was rudely interrupted just as all classes had learned to enjoy the drink and the sociability that accompanied it. One of the most attractive aspects of the struggle for Independence is the devotion of women to the cause, expressed in their giving up tea which had become such a pleasurable part of life. Always resourceful and innovative in the use of foodstuffs, they now made Liberty Tea from the four-leafed loosestrife and Hyperiod tea from raspberry leaves, those growing along the riverbanks of present Maine being judged of particularly good quality. Tea was also made from ribwort, strawberry and currant leaves, sage, and thoroughwart.

How sad and how brave the lady could be was expressed in the following poem:

A Lady's Adieu to her Tea-Table

Farewell the Tea-board with your gaudy attire,
Ye cups and ye saucers that I did admire;
To my cream pot and tongs I now bid adieu;
That pleasure's all fled that I once found in you.
Farewell pretty chest that so lately did shine,
With hyson and congo and best double fine;
Many a sweet moment by you I have sat,
Hearing girls and old maids to tattle and chat;
And the spruce coxcomb laugh at nothing at all,
Only some silly work that might happen to fall.
No more shall my teapot so generous be
In filling the cups with this pernicious tea,
For I'll fill it with water and drink out the same,
Before I'll lose LIBERTY that dearest name . . .[125]

The men too, renounced, suffered and learned new ways. Attorney John Adams, on his court rounds in the District of Maine in July 1774 wrote to Abigail,

> I believe I forgot to tell you one Anecdote: When I first came to this House it was late in the Afternoon, and I had ridden 35 miles at least. "Madam" said I to Mrs. Huston, "is it lawful for a weary Traveller to refresh himself with a Dish of Tea provided it has been honestly smuggled, or paid no Duties?"
> "No Sir, said she, we have renounced all Tea in this place. I can't make Tea, but I'le make you Coffee." Accordingly I have drank Coffee every Afternoon since, and have borne it very well. Tea must be universally renounced. I must be weaned, and the sooner, the better.[126]

Many Americans were won over to coffee during those war years, and tea drinking did not regain its universal popularity. However, in certain groups tea was still part of a graceful way of life. At the Hale Homestead of Coventry, Connecticut the post-Revolutionary tea table is all set. Nathan Hale never lived in this house, the family moving in just a month after he was hung in 1776, just as rumors were reaching Connecticut of the hanging. But the tea party shown at the house took place later, when Nathan's sister Joanna was already married. Her wedding silver is on display in the parlor bureau. The Queen Anne maple tea table is like one that belonged to her mother, and on the table is Joanna's Chinese Export china. In the dining room are some of Joanna's copper kettles. Accompanying the tea might be fruitcake or poundcake, lemon or orange cookies, seed cakes, apples and nuts.

The sociability of the tea party is presented to us in full bloom in the following account of the Salem (Massachusetts) Tea, where China trade brought wealth and Samuel McIntyre brought beauty to the houses, in addition to the ladies who brought grace to everyday life.

The account is by Caroline Howard King, who was born in 1822 and is speaking of fashions of her youth:

"Salem was more famous in those early days for its delightful and cosy tea parties than for any great literary interests . . . They could hardly be called 'aesthetic teas,' for as everybody had dined in the middle of the day, the guests brought good appetites to the feast, and fully enjoyed the dainties set before them . . . We all sat down at a long table (or a round table which was cosier and merrier), upon which was spread a red cloth, or a plaided red, white, and blue one, which threw into high relief the shining silver and glass, and the India blue and gold tea set of the time. There were no tray cloths then. In front of the hostess were placed two highly decorative black and gold Chinese lacquered tea trays. (We called them waiters.) On one were placed silver tea-pots for both green and black tea and the coffee or chocolate pot, and on the other larger one was the urn for hot water, and if the tea was made on the table a dainty silver or lacquer tea caddy, with the sugar bowl, cream pitcher and slop bowl belonging to the tea service and all the nankin china cups and saucers and coffee mugs spread out in shining array. Then plates were placed all down the sides of the table accompanied always by pretty little 'cup plates.' It was the custom of the day to cool your tea before drinking it by pouring it into your saucer, and these small plates were to hold the cup . . . There were no courses at these teas. Everything was put on the bountifully provided table at once. The plates were changed between meats and sweets, but the menu was spread out before you, and if you were not hungry enough to partake of the whole array, you could choose your favorite dainty. At the foot of the table where the host sat was placed the solid part of the feast—cooked oysters and chickens or game dressed in different ways. I once saw a noble chicken pie at one of these teas. Down the middle of the table were silver cake baskets with pound, sponge and fruit cake, and these were flanked on each side by plates and small dishes containing different kinds of bread and hot cakes, olives, tongue, and ham . . . Then there were cut glass dishes of many kinds of preserves, whole quinces floating in their rich clear juice being always present and damsons and preserved ginger . . . Such a table, lighted by plenty of tall silver candlesticks, and surrounded by a jocund company of merry guests, had . . . a glow and brilliancy and an affluent charm which one seldom sees equalled . . . today.''[127]

Other Colonial Beverages

Mention has been made of that ''national'' drink of New England, cider, but there were other beverages served at the home fireside or in the parlor. When pears and peaches were ripe, some colonists made perry and peachy, something akin to cider in the method, but peachy had the most delectable flavor and has been favorably compared to champagne.

Metheglin had a long history and remained a country drink long after colonial days. It was made from yeast, honey and water.

A good summer drink was switchel, made from molasses, water and ginger. It had a reputation for its cooling properties and was served to men in the hayfields for their relief from the hot sun. From this use it came to be called Haymakers' Switchel. A modern version calls for two quarts of water, 1 cup brown sguar, 1/2 cup sweet

Trencher used as bowl, Ironmaster's House.

vinegar, and 1 tsp. ginger.[128] The original was more complicated in the making, and the final product achieved an alcoholic content.

Flip was a considerably more potent drink. Mrs. Earle called it "indescribably burnt and bitter in flavor,"[129] and said she would rather read about it than drink it. This is the drink made from "home-brewed beer, sweetened with sugar, molasses or dried pumpkin, and flavored with a liberal dash of rum, then stirred in a great mug or pitcher with a red-hot logger-head." The loggerhead is a large iron swizzle-stick whose lozenge end was placed in the fire to get hot before it was thrust into the drink, causing it to foam up nicely.

Sack, a white wine, was still drunk in colonial days but was no longer the great favorite it had been in Shakespeare's, or Falstaff's days. Sack-posset was associated with weddings. This was hot milk curdled with sack, spices and sugar. On December 3, 1715 Samuel Sewall went to visit his married daughter "and gave her my Wife's Wedding Ring, saying I hoped she would wear it with the same Nobility as she did who was the first owner of it. While her Husband and I were fitting part of his Sermon for the Press, she came in and gave us excellent Sack-posset. I told her, the Ring I had given her was her Mother's Wedding Ring; and this entertainment Savour'd of a Wedding.''[130] On May 12, 1720 daughter Judith was married and Judge Sewall noted, ''We had our Cake, and Sack-posset.''[131]

Judge Sewall also enjoyed a sillabub on occasion. This was a dish of cream mixed with wine or cider to form a curd. Later it was the style to whip it so that the top had a froth. It would seem to qualify both as a beverage and as a dessert, though it would be eaten with a spoon much as we eat and drink a thick milkshake. The Webb House has a set of sillabub glasses.

> *A Fine Syllabub from the Cow*
> Sweeten a quart of cyder with double refined sugar, grate nutmeg into it, then milk your cow into your liquor. When you have thus added what quantity of milk you think proper, pour half a pint or more, in proportion to the quantity of syllabub you make, of the sweetest cream you can get all over it.

By the late eighteenth century sillabubs were whipped, and we have this recipe from the manuscript recipe book of Mrs. Tallmadge of Litchfield:

> Take a pint of thick cream and half a pint of wine, the juice of two Oranges or Lemons and grate in the peal of two Lemons — half a pound of double refined sugar — switch it well in an earthen pan, then pour a little wine into the glass. Custard — to a quart of new milk put 4 eggs, sweeten to your taste — add spices.

Perhaps the most popular of all social drinks before tea was punch, and a punch bowl was a most desired and cherished belonging. Fashionable dinners began with a bowl of punch passed from hand to hand, guests drinking directly from it. Such a bowl held about a quart. The young Anna Green Winslow was sent from Nova Scotia to live with her aunt and uncle in Boston, where she would receive an education proper for a girl of her station in life. Soon she wrote home to her parents about ''a very genteel well regulated assembly which we had at Mr. Stoley's last evening. . . . There was a large company assembled in a handsome, large, upper room in the new end of the house. We had two fiddles, & I had the honor to open the diversion of the evening in a minuet with miss Soley . . . our treat was nuts, raisins, Cakes, Wine, punch, hot & cold, all in great plenty. We had a very agreeable evening from 5 to 10 o'clock . . . no rudeness Mamma I assure you.''[132]

There should have been no rudeness either at the ordination of the Rev. Joseph McKean in 1785 in Beverly, Massachusetts, but the tavern keeper's bill would leave room for wonder. Eighty people at the morning meal and 68 at dinner consumed:

> 30 bowles of Punch before the People went to meeting
> 44 bowles of punch while at dinner, besides
> 28 bottles of wine and 8 bowls of Brandy
> same amount of Cherry Rum, and 6 people drank tea.

And Governor Hancock gave a dinner in 1792 for 80 Fusileers in Boston. They drank 136 bowls of punch besides sherry, brandy, and cider.

Among the pieces of fireside equipment shown to us, we sometimes see the ale shoe, a container shaped to slip into the embers without spilling the contents and resembling indeed a shoe suitable for the tin man. The Mission House and Buttolph-Williams have these. The latter house also has a leather jack, a tall drinking vessel made of leather which gave rise to the Frenchmen's opinion that the English drank from their boots.

Dairy Foods

Cheesemaking was a buttery, not a fireside, duty, but the cheese press and ladder are so frequently to be seen in museum kitchens and are so baffling to look at that it seems fitting to explain briefly the use of the things.

The housewife saved milk for several days until she had a sufficient quantity. She skimmed off the cream, leaving the milk for cheese. Then she added the rennet, which is a preparation made from the stomach of a butchered calf and is essential in cheesemaking. The rennet caused the curd to form in about an hour. At that point she would cut the amber curd and the whey would separate from it. She dipped off the whey several times and then put the curd into a cloth-lined cheese basket on a ladder with a bowl underneath to catch the remaining whey that drained out. When the draining process was complete, she salted the curd with a teacupful of Liverpool salt to ten pounds, according to an old recipe. Then she put it into the hoop on the base of the press, covered it with the board and set the press.

Here she left it for a day or two, and when she took it out, oiled it with melted butter, wrapped it in cheesecloth and set it to ripen in a cool, dark place. Still she must turn and oil it frequently, ''a considerable task when the cheeses were many, and weighed, as they often did, from 25 to 30 pounds.''[135]

Old Narragansett was famous for its cheeses which were exported to England and the Barbadoes. One of the valued possessions at Richard Smith's ''Castle'' (1678) near Wickford, Rhode Island, is Madam Smith's handwritten receipt for making cheese in the manner of her home district of Cheshire, England. Her directions are essentially those given above, except that she specifies the cheese must be kept on a ''shelf in a dark closet for six months, turning daily rubbing well with butter. Keep from Flies.'' That last direction was not so easily accomplished, and some women laid tansey leaves on their cheeses in a noble effort to ward off the flies.

As for buttermaking, that was a June and September chore. The goodwife set the milk in her keeler overnight, and in the morning skimmed off the cream which she placed in the churn and worked with the dasher until the butter ''came.'' Next she worked it by hand or with a wooden paddle to get out all the buttermilk, then washed it, salted it and packed it away in an earthen jar.

The pride and sense of accomplishment that resulted from these lengthy and laborious chores is symbolized by one small wooden accouterment: the butter pat, a device with which the housewife would stamp a pretty design onto her butter.

Herbs

Outside the door and conveniently close to the kitchen was the herb garden, as necessary to the colonial housewife as any adjunct to her hearth. This was her domain. Husbandman had his fields of grain crops, huswife had her herb garden, where she grew the necessary ingredients for medicines, flavorings, insecticides, and fragrances.

Markham instructed her in what he considered the most important knowledge for the housewife, "a perfect skill" in cookery, the first step toward which was,

> to have knowledge of all sorts of hearbs belonging to the Kitchin, whether they be for the Pot, for Sallets, for Sauces, for Servings, or for any other Seasoning, or adorning; which skill of knowledge of the Hearbs she must get by her owne labour and experience . . . for the use of them, she shall see it in the composition of dishes and meates here-after following. She shall also know the time of the yeere, Month and Moone, in which all Hearbs are to bee sowne; and when they are in their best flourishing, that gathering all Hearbs in their height of goodness, she may have the prime use of the same.[136]

She needed a knowledge of medicinal as well as culinary herbs for nursing her own family in their sicknesses. Such knowledge was as essential as knowing the operation of a spit or an oven. Seeds came from England with the early settlers, and the women readily sought the uses and culture of native plants.

Recipes reveal how much herb flavors were desired in cookery, and truly, one can only wonder at the many herbs used in combination, contrary to today when we desire the delicate addition of one, possibly two, herbs to a dish. Where we call for a "pinch" Markham and Josselyn ask for a "handful" or a "faggot"—and then follows a long list of herbs.

The location of the garden near the kitchen was more than a matter of convenience. Rue, tany, and southernwood at the doorstep helped somewhat in keeping ants and flies away. Also, the fragrance of lavendar, marigold, germander, hyssop and the thymes might drift into the house.

Many of our restored historic houses in New England have been treated to a dooryard garden by their local garden club or an arm of their historical society. The reconstructed houses at Plimoth Plantation have their herb and vegetable gardens. The Ashley House has the attractive goosefoot design for its herb garden. In Wethersfield the Stevens House has an herb garden, while next door the Webb House has an old-fashioned flower garden. The garden at the Mission House in Stockbridge is very large, but removed somewhat from the door because there is a magnificently old and large grape arbor by the back door. The Whipple House in Ipswich has a garden designed by Arthur A. Shurcliff, who also designed the gardens at the Governor's Palace at Williamsburg. The Whipple garden was planted by Mrs. A.W. Smith of Ipswich, who, under the pen name of Ann Leighton, is the author of *Early American Gardens*. This garden consists of six raised beds about ten feet square. Every one of the eighty or more plants used in the beds is known to have been used by the seventeenth century housewife, as evidenced by contemporary documents. The garden paths are white with local clamshells ground fine through use.

The herb garden is the place to end your visit to an Early American house, the place where you can let what you have just seen in the house take root in your memory and imagination, where you can make the transition gradually from colonial times back to the present. Here we also leave the colonial housewife taking a rest among the ''simples'' of her garden, finding here balm for her spirit.

Historic Houses Open to the Public

(Hours vary and some are closed during the winter, so check before going.)

Antiquarian House (1809), Plymouth, Mass.
Eleazer Arnold House (1687), Lincoln, R.I.
Col. Ashley House (1735), Ashley Falls, Mass.
John Balch House (1636), Beverly, Mass.
Bates-Scofield House (1736) Darien, Conn.
Sylvanus Brown House (1758), Slater Mill Historic Site, Pawtucket, R.I.
Bush-Holley House (1685), Cos Cob, Conn.
Abraham Browne, Jr. House (1690), Watertown, Mass.
Buttolph-Williams House (1692), Wethersfield, Conn.
Parson Capen House (1683), Topsfield, Mass.
Claflin-Richards House (1663/4), Wenham, Mass.
Clemence—Irons House (c. 1680), Johnston, R.I.
Jethro Coffin House (1686), Nantucket, Mass.
Tristram Coffin House (1654), Newbury, Mass.
Crowninshield-Bentley House (1729), Essex Institute, Salem, Mass.
Daggett House (1695), Slater Park, Pawtucket, R.I.
Josiah Day House (1754), West Springfield, Mass.
Silas Deane House (1766), Wethersfield, Conn.
Jonathan Dickerman House (1770), Hamden, Conn.
Justice Oliver Ellsworth House (1740), Windsor, Conn.
Fairbanks House (1636), Dedham, Mass.
Fyler House (1640), Windsor, Conn.
Glebe House (1690/1750), Woodbury, Conn.
Thomas Griswold House (1735), Guilford, Conn.
Hawthorne Birthplace (1692/1750), House of Seven Gables Complex,
    Salem, Mass.
Hale Homestead (1776), Coventry, Conn.
Rev. John Hale House (1694), Beverly, Mass.
Harlow/Old Fort House (1677), Plymouth, Mass.
Hempsted House (1678/1728), New London, Conn.

121

Hurd House (c. 1680), Woodbury, Conn.
Hyland House (1660/1720), Guilford, Conn.
Ironmaster's House (1650), National Historic Site, Saugus, Mass.
Jackson House (1664), Portsmouth, N.H.
Jefferds Tavern (1750), York Village, Maine.
Judson House (1723), Stratford, Conn.
Keeler Tavern (1772), Ridgefield, Conn.
Thomas Lee House (1660), Niantic, Conn.
Leffingwell Inn (1675), Norwich, Conn.
Mission House/Rev. John Sargeant (1739), Stockbridge, Mass.
Rebecca Nurse House (1600's), Danvers, Conn.
Pardee-Morris House (1679/1780), New Haven, Conn.
Lady Pepperell House (1760), Kittery Point, Maine.
Phelps House (1771), Massacoe Plantation, Simsbury, Conn.
Putnam Cottage (1690), Greenwich, Conn.
Rider House (1785), Scott-Fanton Museum, Danbury, Conn.
House of the Seven Gables (1668), Salem, Mass.
Shaw Mansion (1756), New London, Conn.
Sheldon-Hawkes House (1743), Deerfield, Mass.
Smith's Castle at Cocumscussoc, Wickford, R.I.
Stanley-Whitman House/Farmington Museum (1660/1760), Farmington, Conn.
Isaac Stevens House (1788), Wethersfield, Conn.
Strawbery Banke Houses: Portsmouth, N.H.
    Capt. John Sherburne (c. 1695/1703)
    Capt. John Clarke (c. 1750)
    Capt. Keyran Walsh (c. 1796)
Stencil House (1790), Shelburn Museum, Burlington, Vt.
Gilbert Stuart Birthplace (1750), Saunderstown, R.I.
Swett-Ilsey House/Blue Onion Tavern (1670/1720), Newbury, Mass.
Gov. Jonathan Trumbull House (1740), Lebanon, Conn.
Wanton-Lyman-Hazard House (pre-1700), Newport, R.I.
John Ward House (1684), Essex Institute, Salem, Mass.
Joseph Webb House (1752), Wethersfield, Conn.
Noah Webster Birthplace (pre-1758), West Hartford, Conn.
Wells-Shipman-Ward House (1755), South Glastonbury, Conn.
Wentworth-Gardner House (1760), Portsmouth, N.H.
Whipple House (1640/1670), Ipswich, Mass.
Henry Whitfield House (1639), Guilford, Conn.

Footnotes

1 Edward Johnson, *Wonder-Working Providence of Sions Savior in New England* (London, 1654: reprint ed., Delmar, New York: Scholars' Facsimiles and Reprints, 1974), p. 174.

2 Norman M. Isham and Albert F. Brown, *Early Rhode Island Houses: An Historical and Architectural Study* (Providence: Preston and Rounds, 1895), p. 16.

3 Johnson, *op. cit.*, p. 174.

4 William Bradford: *Of Plymouth Plantation: The Pilgrims in America*, ed. and with an introduction by Harvey Wish (New York: Capricorn Books, 1962), p. 52.

5 Trustees of the Henry Whitfield Museum, *The Henry Whitfield House* (n.p., n.d.), p. 12.

6 Joshua Coffin, letter to his father, quoted in *The Tristram Coffin House* (Collectaguide Historic House Folder, Collectaguide Company, 1939), p. 2.

7 Deputy Gov. Samuel Symonds, letter to Gov. Winthrop, quoted in Sherman L. Whipple and Thomas Franklin Waters, *Puritan Homes* (No. XXVII, Publications of the Ipswich Historical Society, 1929), p. 20.

8 Trustees of the Henry Whitfield Museum, *op. cit.*, p. 12.

9 Dr. Elijah Woodward, "Reminiscences," (undocumented newspaper clipping, Watertown (Conn.) Historical Society Scrapbook #6, File B-2), unpaged.

10 Frances Phipps, *Colonial Kitchens, Their Furnishings and Their Gardens* (New York: Hawthorn Books, 1972), p. 94.

11 Interview with James Baker, Director, Plimoth Plantation, Plymouth, Massachusetts, 8 September 1978.

12 Sherman L. Whipple and Thomas Franklin Waters, *Puritan Homes* (No. XXVII, Publications of the Ipswich Historical Society, 1929), p. 32 f.

13 Jane deForest Shelton, *The Salt-Box House: Eighteenth Century Life in a New England Hill Town* (New York: Baker and Taylor Company, 1900), p. 94.

14 All Higley Inventories from the Probate Court Records, Connecticut State Library, Hartford, Conn.

15 Phipps, *op. cit.*, p. 54.

16 Abigail Foote "Journal," Entry for 9 June 1775 (collections of Connecticut Historical Society, Hartford, Connecticut).

17 Cutler Dothe (Stone) Mrs. Younglove. "Diary, 1777–1792, (ms copy, Litchfield Historical Society). Entry 30 June 1784.

18 Jay Allen Anderson, "A Solid Sufficiency: An Ethnography of Yeoman Foodways in Stuart England" (Ph.D. dissertation, University of Pennsylvania, 1971), p. 234.

19 *Ibid.*, p. 234, with internal quotation Laslett, *The World We Have Lost* (London, 1965), p. 15.

20 Thomas Tusser, *Five hundred Points of Good Husbandry together with a Book of Huswifery* (London 1557, reprinted 1612) quoted in Anderson, *op. cit.*, p. 240.

21 Samuel Eliot Morison, *Three Centuries of Harvard: 1636–1936* (Cambridge: Harvard University Press, 1936), p 27 f.

22 Samuel Sewall, *Diary*, ed. Mark Van Doren (n.p. Macy-Masius, 1927), p. 48.

23 *Ibid.*, p. 175.

24 Patricia Easterbrook Roberts, *Table Settings, Entertaining, and Etiquette: A History and Guide* (New York: Bonanza Books, n.d.), p. 202.

25 Timothy Dwight, *Travels in New England and New York*, The John Harvard Library, Vol. IV (Cambridge: Belknap Press of Harvard University Press, 1969), p. 250.

26 Samuel Griswold Goodrich, *Recollections of a Lifetime . . .* Vol. 1 (New York and Auburn, Miller, Orton & Mulligan, 1856), p. 83-4.

27 *Henry Wansey and His American Journal: 17f4*, ed. David John Jeremy (Philadelphia: American Philosophical Society, 1970), p. 57.

28 George L. Clark, *History of Connecticut* (New York: G.P. Putnam, 1914).

29 Lyman Beecher, D.D., *Autobiography, Correspondence, Etc.*, Vol. 1, ed. Charles Beecher (New York: Harper and Brothers, 1865), p. 27.

30 Goodrich, *op. cit.*, p. 83 f.

31 Charles Francis Adams, *Three Episodes of Massachusetts* Vol. II (Boston and New York: Houghton, Mifflin & Co., 1923), p. 686.

32 Adams, *op. cit.*, p. 806.

33 Beecher, *op. cit.*, p. 27

34 Dwight, *op. cit.*, p. 249

35 Samuel Eliot Morison, *The Maritime History of Massachusetts* (Boston: Houghton Mifflin Co., 1941), p. 147.

36 Sarah Kemble Knight, *The Private Journal of, Being the Record of a Journey from Boston to New York in the Year 1704* (Norwich, Conn.: The Academy Press, 1901), n.p. Entry for 7 October 1704.

37 Alice Morse Earle, *Home Life in Colonial Days* (New York: Grosset and Dunlap, 1898), p. 81.

38 Edith Minter, "When Treen Ware was 'The Ware,'" *Antiques*, December 1930, p. 504 ff.

39 Manchester *Guardian*, undated clipping in collection of Plymouth Antiquarian Society.

40 Joseph B. Starshak, "Dining in Deerfield: A Cultural Index" (Heritage Foundation study, Historic Deerfield, 1965), p. 5.

41 *Ibid.*, p. 5.

42 The Rev. Francis Higginson, *New England's Plantation* (London: T. & R. Cotes, 1630, reproduced by the New England Society in the City of New York, 1930), last page, no number.

43 Beecher, *op. cit.*, p. 27.

44 Thomas Danforth Boardman, *Autobiography*, quoted in Charles F. Montgomery, *A History of American Pewter* (New York: Praeger, 1973), p. 7.

45 Samuel Eliot Morison, *Three Centuries of Harvard: 1636–1936* (Cambridge: Harvard University Press, 1936), p. 20.

46 Boston Town Records, 1660–1700, in *Report of the Record Commissioners of the City of Boston*, ed. William H. Whitmore, Vol. 7 (Published by the City of Boston, 1881, p. 134), quoted in Montgomery, *op. cit.*, p. 10.

47 Montgomery, *op. cit.*, p. 22.

48 Joshua Hempstead, *Diary . . . covering a Period of Forty-seven years from Sept. 1711 to Nov. 1758* (New London: The New London Historical Society, 1901), p. 418, entry 25 Nov. 1743.

49 *Ibid.*, p. 418, entry 3 Dec. 1743.

50 *Connecticut Courant*, No. 134, 20 July 1767, p. 4.

51 Montgomery, *op. cit.*, p. 14.

52 *Ibid.*, p. 121.

53 R.B. Bailey, *Pilgrim Possessions as told by Their Wills and Inventories* (mimeographed copy provided by Plimoth Plantation, no documentation), p. 9 of mimio.

54 John Spargo, *Early American Pottery and China* (New York and London: The Century Company, 1926), p. 54.

55 N. Hudson Moore, *Delftware: Dutch and English* (New York: Frederick A. Stokes Co., 1908), p. 7 f.

56 *Ibid.*, p. 63.

57 Spargo, *op. cit.*, p. 64.

58 James Deetz, *In Small Things Forgotten: The Archeology of Early American Life* (Garden City: Anchor Press/Doubleday, 1907), p. 124 f.

59 Susannah Carter, *The Frugal Housewife: or complete woman cook* (Philadelphia: Carey, 1796, microfilm Evans #30168), n.p.

60 *Ibid.*, n.p.

61 George Ursal, "Cooking in Colonial Boston," *Early American Life*, October 1976, p. 24.

62 John Adams to Abigail Adams, quoted in Helen Sprackling, *Customs on the Table Top* (Sturbridge: Old Sturbridge Village, 1958), p. 19.

63 John Adams, Diary entry, quoted in Catherine Drinker Bowen, *John Adams and the American Revolution* (Boston: Little, Brown and Co., 1950), p. 466.

64 John Adams, quoted in Charles Francis Adams, *Works of John Adams, Second President of the United States* (Boston: Charles C. Little and James Brown, 1850), Vol. II, p. 342.

65 Dwight, *op. cit.*, p. 250

66 James Deetz and Jay Anderson, *Partakers of Plenty* (Plimoth Plantation Educational Publication, reprint of "The Ethnogastronomy of Thanksgiving," *Saturday Review of Science*, November 25, 1972, 4th page, unnumbered.

67 Edward Winslow, Letter to a friend . . . 11 December 1621.

68 Higginson, *op. cit.*, pages unnumbered.

69 *Ibid.*, n.p.

70 *Ibid.*, n.p.

71 Wood, *op. cit.*, p. 11 f.

72 Capt. Roger Clap, *Memoirs* (Boston: printed for William Tileston Clap by David Carlisle, 1807, first printed Boston: T. Prince, 1731), p. 23.

73 Peter Stone, *1776* (New York: Viking Press, 1964), Sc. 7, p. 115.

74 *Boston News-Letter*, 7/14 December 1732.

75 *Boston News-Letter*, 28 April 1768.

76 *Connecticut Courant*, 25 July 1768.

77 *Connecticut Courant*, 25 July 1768.

78 *Boston Gazette*, 19 September 1752.

79 Joel Barlow, *The Hasty Pudding* (New Haven: 1796. Microfilm Evans #30022).

80 Morison, *Three Centuries* . . . , p. 182.

81 Thomas Robinson Hazard, *The Jonny-Cake Papers of "Shepherd Tom"* (Boston: for the Subscribers, 1915), p. 23 f.

82 *Ibid.*, p. 29.

83 *Ibid.*, p. 27.

84 Anonymous, "Our Forefathers' Song," *The Art of American Humor*, ed. Brom Weber (New York: Thomas Y. Crowell), p. 13 f.

85 Josselyn, quoted in Earle, *Customs*, p. 151.

86 Knight, *op. cit.*, unnumbered pages.

87 John Josselyn, *New England's Rarities* (London: 1672, reprinted Boston: William Veazie, 1965), p. 109.

88 Samuel Deane, *The New England Farmer* (Worcester: Isaiah Thomas, 1790), p. 224.

89 Edwin Valentine Mitchell, *It's an Old State of Maine Custom* (New York: Vanguard Press, 1949), p. 116.

90 Dr. Aikin, *The Arts of Life* (Boston: Hosea Sprague, 1803), p. 15.

91 Earle, *Customs*, p. 153.

92 Peter Kalm, *Travels into North America*, trans. John Reinhold Forster (Barre, Mass.: The Imprint Society, 1972), p. 98.

93 Johnson, *op. cit.*, p. 175.

94 Hempstead, *op. cit.*, p. 445.

95 Peter Wynne, *Apples* (New York: Hawthorn Books, Inc., 1975), p. 54 f.

96 Miss Mary Russell, "A Young English Girl's Diary while residing at Middletown, Ct., with her father at the end of the Eighteenth Century, Nov. 1796 till Apr. 1801." "An exact copy," typed ms. Col. Conn. Historical Society.

97 Abigail Foote, "Journal," Conn. Historical Society.

98 Josselyn, *Rarities*, p. 113.

99 Alma DeForest Curtiss, Recipe Book, holograph notebook, 1839. Courtesy the Watertown Library Association, Watertown, Ct.

100 Earle, *Customs*, p. 155.

101 Josselyn, quoted in *A Plimoth Colony Cook Book*, p. 78. (no further source given.)

102 G.M. (Gervase Markham), *Countrey Contentments, or the English Huswife* . . . (London: 1615, reprint London: 1623), p. 60.

103 J. Murrell, *Two Books of Cookery and Carving*, 1650, quoted in Mary Mac-Nicol, *Flower Cookery* (N.Y.: Macmillan, 1972).

104 Bradford, *op. cit.*, p. 101 and 130.

105 Josselyn, quoted in Ann Leighton, *Early American Gardens "For Meate or Medicine"* (Boston: Houghton Mifflin Co., 1970), p. 110 f.

106 Markham, *op. cit.*, p. 71 f.

107 *Ibid.*, p. 90.

108 Dwight, *op. cit.*, p. 249.

109 Mrs. (Lydia Maria) Child, *The American Frugal Housewife*, 12th ed. (Boston: Carter, Hendee, & Co., 1833, facsimile ed. printed for Worthington, Ohio, Historical Society, 1965), p. 66.

110 Amelia Simmons, *American Cookery* . . . (1796 reprint ed. Grand Rapids, Michigan: William B. Eerdmans Publishing Co., 1965), p. 42.

111 Edward Augustus Kendall, *Travels Through the Northern Parts of the United States in the Years 1807-1808* (New York, 1809).

112 Courtesy the Wells-Shipman-Ward House Recipe Tasting, 15 October 1978.

113 Mrs. Rev. Frederick Holcomb, *Watertown Reminiscences*.

114 In *Love's Labours Lost*, V, i, 66-7, and "The Idle 'Prentice.'"

115 Goodrich, *op. cit.*, p. 68.

116 Wansey, *op. cit.*, p. 69.

117 John Burroughs.

118 Johnson, *op. cit.*, p. 175.

119 John Josselyn, *An Account of Two Voyages to New England* (London: 1675, from *Collections* of the Massachusetts Historical Society, Vol. III of the Third Series, Cambridge: E.W. Metcalf & Co., 1833, pp. 211-396), p. 221.

120 Louise C. Belden, "The Colonial Dessert Table," *Antiques*, December 1975, p. 1162, nt. 5.

121 *Ibid.*, p. 1157.

122 Markham, *op. cit.*, p. 112.

123 See especially "Family Group" by Gawen Hamilton, c. 1730, in collection of Colonial Williamsburg, reproduced in Roth, *Tea Drinking*, q.v.

124 Rodris Roth, *Tea Drinking in Eighteenth Century America: Its Etiquette and Equipage*, (United States National Museum Bulletin 225, Paper 14 from Contributions from the Museum of History and Technology, Washington, D.C.: Smithsonian Institution, 1961), p. 84.

125 *Ibid.*, p. 68.

126 John Adams to Abigail Adams, 6 July 1774, quoted in *The Book of Abigail and John: Selected Letters of the Adams Family: 1762-1784*, ed. L.H. Butterfield, Marc Friedlaender and Mary-Jo Kline (Cambridge and London: Harvard University Press, 1975), p. 61.

127 Caroline Howard King, *When I Lived in Salem: 1822–1866.* (Brattleboro, Vt.: Stephen Daye Press, 1937), p. 104 ff.

128 Eric Sloane, *Seasons of America Past* (New York: Wilfred Funk, Inc., 1958), p. 68.

129 Alice Morse Earle, *Colonial Dames and Good Wives* (Boston and New York: Houghton, Mifflin & Co., 1895), p. 286.

130 Sewall, *op. cit.,* p. 236.

131 *Ibid.,* p. 250.

132 Anna Green Winslow, *Diary of: A Boston School Girl of 1771,* ed. Alice Morse Earle (Detroit: Singing Tree Press, 1970), p. 16 f.

133 Simmons, *op. cit.,* p. 42.

134 Knight, *op. cit.,* entry for 7 October 1704.

135 Charles Shepherd Phelps, *Rural Life in Litchfield County* (Norfolk, Conn.: The Litchfield County University Club, 1917), p. 76 f.

136 Markham, *op. cit.,* p. 57.

Bibliography

Adams, Charles Francis. *Three Episodes of Massachusetts History.* Vol. II. Boston and New York: Houghton, Mifflin and Co., 1923.

Aikin, Dr. *The Arts of Life.* Boston: Hosea Sprague, 1803.

Anderson, Jay Allen. "A Solid Sufficiency: An Ethnography of Yeoman Foodways in Stuart England." A Ph.D. Dissertation. The University of Pennsylvania, 1971.

Architecture on the Piscataqua. Portsmouth, New Hampshire: Strawbery Banke, Inc., 1964.

Aresty, Esther B. *The Delectable Past.* New York: Simon and Shuster, 1964.

Bailey, R.B. "Pilgrim Possessions as told by Their Wills and Inventories." Mimeograph. Plimoth Plantation.

Barlow, Joel. The Hasty Pudding. New Haven: 1796. Microfilm, Evans #30022.

Beecher, Lyman. *Autobiography, Correspondence, Etc.* Vol. 1. Edited by Charles Beecher. New York: Harper and Bros., 1865.

Belden, Louise C. "The Colonial Dessert Table." *Antiques,* December 1975, pp. 1156–1163.

Book of Abigail and John, The: Selected Letters of the Adams Family: 1762–1784. Edited by L.H. Butterfield, March Friedlaender and Mary-Jo Kline. Cambridge, Mass., and London, England: Harvard University Press, 1975.

Boston News-Letter. 7/14 Dec. 1732; 28 April 1768.

Boston Gazette. 19 Sept. 1752.

Bowen, Catherine Drinker. *John Adams and the American Revolution.* Boston: Little, Brown and Co., 1950.

Bradford, William. *Of Plymouth Plantation: The Pilgrims in America.* Edited by Harvey Wish. New York: Capricorn Books, 1962.

Bradley, Robert L. *Maine's First Buildings: The Architecture of Settlement, 1604–1700.* Maine Historic Preservation Commission, 1976.

Brett, Gerard. *Dinner is Served: A Study in Manners.* Hamden. Conn.: Archon Books, 1969.

Carter, Susanna. *The Frugal Housewife*. Boston: Edes and Gill, 1772. Microfilm, Evans #12348.

Carter, Susannah. *The Frugal Housewife: or complete woman cook*. Philadelphia: Carey, 1796. Microfilm, Evans #30168.

Child, Mrs. (Lydia Maria). *The American Frugal Housewife*. 12th ed. Boston: Carter, Hendee, and Co., 1833. Facsimile edition printed for Worthington, Ohio, Historical Society, 1965.

Clap, Capt. Roger. *Memoirs*. Boston: T. Prince, 1731. Reprinted for William Tileston Clap. Boston: David Carlisle, 1807.

Clark, George L. *History of Connecticut*. New York: G.P. Putnam, 1914.

Congdon, Herbert Wheaton. *Old Vermont Houses*. Brattleboro: Stephen Daye Press, 1940.

Connecticut Courant, 25 July 1768.

Curtiss, Alma DeForest. Recipe Book. Holygraph notebook, 1839. In possession of Watertown (Conn.) Library Association.

Cutler, Dothe (Stone) Mrs. Younglove. Diary, 1777–1792. Copy in possession of Litchfield Historical Society.

Davidson, Marshall B.*Our Medieval Heritage*. Reprinted form Marshall B. Davidson, *The American Heritage History of Colonial Antiques*. American Heritage Publishing Co., 1967. A Plimoth Plantation Reprint.

Deane, Samuel. *The New England Farmer*. Worcester: Isaiah Thomas, 1790.

Deetz, James. *In Small Things Forgotten: The Archeology of Early American Life*. Garden City: Anchor Press/Doubleday, 1977.

Deetz, James, and Anderson, Jay. *Partakers of Plenty*. A Plimoth Plantation Education Publication. Reprint of "The Ethnogastronomy of Thanksgiving," *Saturday Review of Science*, 25 November 1972.

Dow, George Francis. *Domestic Life in New England in the Seventeenth Century*. A Discourse. New York: Benjamin Blom, 1972. Reissue of 1925 printing.

Dow, George Francis. *Every Day Life in the Massachusetts Bay Colony*. Boston: The Society for the Preservation of New England Antiquities, 1935.

Dwight, Timothy. *Travels in New England and New York*. Vol. IV: John Harvard Library. Cambridge: Belknap Press of Harvard University Press, 1969.

Earle, Alice Morse. *Colonial Dames and Good Wives*. Boston and New York: Houghton, Mifflin & Co., 1895.

Earle, Alice Morse. *Customs and Fashions in Old New England*. New York: Charles Scribners, 1893. Reprinted Rutland, Vermont: Charles E. Tuttle, 1973.

Earle, Alice Morse. *Home Life in Colonial Days*. New York: Grosset and Dunlap, 1898.

Elverson, Virginia T. and McLaraban, Mary Ann. *A Cooking Legacy*. New York: Walker and Co., 1975.

Emerson, Lucy. *The New England Cookery*. Montpelier: Josiah Parks, 1808.

Foote, Abigail. Journal. In possession of Conn. Historical Society.

Benjamin Franklin on the Art of Eating together with the Rules of Health and Long Life . . . Printed for the American Philosophical Society by the Princeton University Press, 1958.

Franklin, Benjamin. *The Writings of.* Collected and edited, with Life and Introduction by Albert Henry Smith. Vol. IV: 1760–1766. New York: Macmillan, 1906.

Glass, Hannah. *The Art of Cookery Made Plain and Easy.* London: 1796. With a New Introduction by Fanny Cradock. Hamden, Conn.: Archon Books, 1971.

Goodrich, S.G. (Samuel Griswold). *Recollections of a Lifetime* . . . 2 Vols. New York and Auburn: Miller, Orton and Mulligan, 1856.

Harrison, Molly. *The Kitchen in History.* New York: Charles Scribner's Sons, 1972.

Hawkins, Nancy and Arthur, and Havemeyer, Mary Ellen. *Nantucket and other New England Cooking.* New York: Hastings House, 1976.

Hazard, Thomas Robinson. *The Jonny-Cake Papers of "Shepherd Tom."* With a Biographical Sketch and Notes by Rowland Gibson Hazard. Boston: Printed for the Subscribers, 1915.

Hempstead, Joshua. *Diary* . . . *covering a Period of Forty-seven years from Sept. 1711 to Nov. 1758.* New London: The New London Historical Society, 1901.

Higginson, The Rev. Francis. *New England's Plantation.* London: T. & R. Cotes, 1630. Reproduced by the New England Society in the City of New York, 1930.

Isham, Norman M., and Brown, Albert F. *Early Rhode Island Houses: An Historical and Architectural Study.* Providence: Preston and Rounds, 1895.

Johnson, Edward. *Wonder-Working Providence of Sions Savior in New England* (1654) and *Good News from New England* (1648). Fascimile Reproductions with an introduction by Edward J. Gallagher. Delmar, New York: Scholars' Fascimiles and Reprints, 1974.

Josselyn, John. *An Account of Two Voyages to New England.* London: 1675. Vol. III of the Third Series: *Collections of the Massachusetts Historical Society.* Cambridge: E.W. Metcalf and Co., 1833. pp. 211–396.

Josselyn, John. *New England's Rarities Discovered in Birds, Beasts, Fishes, Serpents, and Plants of that Country.* London: 1672. With an Introduction and Notes by Edward Tuckerman. Boston: William Veazie, 1965.

Kalm, Peter (Pehr). *Travels into North America.* Translated by John Reinhold Forster. Barre, Mass.: The Imprint Society, 1972.

Kauffman, Henry J. *The American Fireplace.* New York: Galahad Books, 1972.

Kendall, Edward Augustus. *Travels Through the Northern Parts of the United States in the Years 1807 and 1808.* New York: 1809.

King, Caroline Howard. *When I Lived In Salem: 1822–1866.* Preface by Louisa L. Dresel. Brattleboro, Vermont: Stephen Daye Press, 1937.

Knight, Sarah Kemble. *The Private Journal of, Being the Record of a Journey from Boston to New York in the Year 1704.* Norwich, Conn.: The Academy Press, MCMI. Limited to 210 copies.

Ladd, Paul. *Early American Fireplaces.* New York: Hastings House, 1977.

Langseth-Christensen, Lillian (with the cooperation of the Marine Historical Association, Inc.) *The Mystic Seaport Cookbook: 350 years of New England Cooking.* New York: Galahad Books, 1970.

Langdon, William Chauncy. *Everyday Things in American Life: 1607–1776.* New York and London: Charles Scribner's Sons, 1937.

Lehman, Rebecca. "The Spoon Speaks Out: Eating Utensils in Deerfield Inventories, 1674–1800. Historic Deerfield Summer Fellowship Program, 1974.

Leighton, Ann (Mrs. A.W. Smith). *Early American Gardens "for Meate or Medicine."* Boston: Houghton Mifflin Co., 1970.

Leslie, Miss. *The House Book or, A Manual of Domestic Economy.* 7th Ed. Philadelphia: Carey and Hart, 1844.

Lindsay, J. Seymour. *Iron and Brass Implements of the English House.* London: Alec Tiranti, 1964.

MacNicol, Mary. *Flower Cookery.* New York: Macmillan, 1972.

G.M. (Gervase Markham). *Countrey Contentments, or the English Huswife.* London: 1615. Reprinted London: 1623.

Miller, Amelia F. *The Rev. Jonathan Ashley House.* Deerfield: Heritage Foundation, c962.

Miniter, Edith. "When Treen Ware was 'The' Ware." *Antiques,* December 1930. pp. 504–507.

Mitchell, Edwin Valentine. *It's An Old State of Maine Custom.* New York: Vanguard Press, 1949.

Montgomery, Charles F. *A History of American Pewter.* (A Winterthur Book). New York and Washington: Praeger Publishers, 1973.

Moore, N. Hudson. *Delftware: Dutch and English.* New York: Frederick A. Stokes Co., 1908.

Morison, Samuel Eliot. *The Maritime History of Massachusetts.* Boston: Houghton Mifflin, 1941.

Morison, Samuel Eliot. *Three Centuries of Harvard: 1636–1936.* Cambridge: Harvard University Press, 1936.

Oldport Cooks. Recipes from the Open Hearth of the Wanton-Lyman-Hazard House. Newport, R.I. n.d.

Orton, Vrest. *The American Cider Book.* New York: Farrar, Straus and Giroux, 1973.

Perl, Lila. *Red Flannel Hash and Shoo-fly Pie: American Regional Foods and Festivals.* Cleveland and New York: World Publishing Co., 1965.

Phelps, Charles Shepherd. *Rural Life in Litchfield County.* Norfolk, Conn.: The Litchfield County University Club, 1917.

Phipps, Frances. *Colonial Kitchens, Their Furnishings and Their Gardens.* New York: Hawthorn Books, Inc., 1972.

Plimoth Colony Cook Book. Edited by Sally Larkin Erath. Plymouth: Plymouth Antiquarian Society, n.d.

Roberts, Patricia Easterbrook. *Table Settings, Entertaining, and Etiquette: A History and Guide.* New York: Bonanza Books, n.d.

Roberts, Robert. *The House Servant's Directory.* Fascimile of the 1827 edition. Foreword by Charles A. Hammond. Waltham, Mass. for The Gore Place Society, 1977.

Root, Waverley, and deRochemont, Richard. *Eating in America: A History.* New York: William Morrow and Company, 1976.

Roth, Rodris. *Tea Drinking in 18th Century America: Its Etiquette and Equipage.* United States National Museum Bulletin 225. Contributions from the Museum of History and Technology Paper 14. Washington, D.C.: Smithsonian Institution, 1961.

Rundell, Maria Eliza. *New System of Domestic Cookery,* 2nd ed. Boston, 1807. Microfilm, Evans #14014.

Russell, Miss Mary. A Young English Girl's Diary while residing at Middletown, Ct., with her father at the end of the Eighteenth Century. Nov. 1796 till Apr. 1801. An exact copy. (typed). In collections of Conn. Historical Society.

Samuel Sewall's Diary. Edited by Mark van Doren. n.p. Macy-Masius, 1927.

1776, A Musical Play. Book by Peter Stone. New York: Viking Press, 1964.

Shelton, Jane deForest. *The Salt-Box House: Eighteenth Century Life in a New England Hill Town.* New York: The Baker and Taylor Co., 1900.

Silitch, Clarissa M. *The Old Farmer's Almanac Colonial Cookbook.* Dublin, N.H.: Yankee, Inc., 1976.

Simmons, Amelia, an American Orphan. *American Cookery . . . 1796.* Reprint edition. Grand Rapids, Michigan: William B. Eerdmans Publishing Co., 1965.

Sloane, Eric. *Seasons of America Past.* New York: Wilfred Funk, 1958.

Spargo, John. *Early American Pottery and China.* New York and London: The Century Co., 1926.

Sprackling, Heen. *Customs on the Table Top.* Sturbridge, Mass.: Old Sturbridge Village, 1958.

Stamm, Sarah B.B. *et al. Yankee Magazine's Favorite New England Recipes.* Dublin, N.H.: Yankee, Inc., 1972.

Starshak, Joseph B. "Dining in Deerfield: A Cultural Index." Deerfield, Mass.: Heritage Foundation. 24 August 1965.

Stevens, William Oliver. *Nantucket—The Far-Away Island.* New York: Dodd, Mead, & Co., 1966.

Tallmadge, Mary (Floyd) Mrs. Benjamin. "Receipts for Sundries." Holygraph cook book, 1790–1800. In collection of Litchfield Historical Society.

Tusser, Thomas. *Five hundred Points of Good Husbandry together with a Book of Huswifery set forth by Thomas Tusser, Gent^{mn}.* A new edition. London: 1812. (Originally published 1557).

Ursal, George, "Cooking in Colonial Boston," *Early American Life.* October, 1976.

Henry Wansey and His American Journal, 1794. Edited by David John Jeremy. Philadelphia: American Philosophical Society, 1970.

Waters, Thomas Franklin. *Ipswich in the Massachusetts Bay Colony.* Ipswich, Mass.: Ipswich Historical Society, 1905.

Weber, Brom, Editor. The Art of American Humor. New York: Apollo, 1970. p. 13–14.

Whipple, Sherman L. and Waters, Thomas Franklin. *Puritan Homes.* Publications of the Ipswich Historical Society, SSVII. Salem: Newcomb and Gauss for the Historical Society, 1929.

Whitehill, Jane. *Food, Drink, and Recipes of Early New England.* Sturbridge, Mass.: Old Sturbridge Village, 1976.

Willison, George F. *Saints and Strangers.* New York: Reynal and Hitchcock, 1945.

Wilson, Mary Tolford. "Amelia Simmons Fills a Need: *American Cookery, 1796.*" *William and Mary Quarterly*, 3rd ser. Vol.. XIV, No. 1 (January 1957), pp. 16–30.

Winslow, Anna Green. *Diary of A Boston School Girl of 1771.* Edited by Alice Morse Earle. Detroit: Singing Tree Press, 1970.

Wolcott, Imogene. *The Yankee Cook Book.* New York: Ives, Washburn, Inc. rev. ed. 1971.

Wood, William. *New England's Prospect.* London: Tho. Cotes, 1635.

Wynne, Peter. *Apples.* New York: Hawthorne Books, Inc., 1975.

Zook, Nicholas. *Houses of New England Open to the Public.* Barre, Mass.: Barre Publishers, 1968.